PENGUIN BOOKS — GREAT IDEAS

An Appeal to the Toiling, Oppressed and
Exhausted Peoples of Europe

Leon Trotsky

1879–1940

Leon Trotsky

*An Appeal to the Toiling,
Oppressed and Exhausted
Peoples of Europe*

PENGUIN BOOKS — GREAT IDEAS

PENGUIN BOOKS

Published by the Penguin Group
Penguin Books Ltd, 80 Strand, London WC2R ORL, England
Penguin Group (USA) Inc., 375 Hudson Street, New York, New York 10014, USA
Penguin Group (Canada), 90 Eglinton Avenue East, Suite 700, Toronto, Ontario, Canada M4P 2Y3
(a division of Pearson Penguin Canada Inc.)
Penguin Ireland, 25 St Stephen's Green, Dublin 2, Ireland (a division of Penguin Books Ltd)
Penguin Group (Australia), 250 Camberwell Road, Camberwell, Victoria 3124, Australia
(a division of Pearson Australia Group Pty Ltd)
Penguin Books India Pvt Ltd, 11 Community Centre, Panchsheel Park, New Delhi – 110 017, India
Penguin Group (NZ), 67 Apollo Drive, Rosedale, North Shore 0632, New Zealand
(a division of Pearson New Zealand Ltd)
Penguin Books (South Africa) (Pty) Ltd, 24 Sturdee Avenue, Rosebank, Johannesburg 2196, South Africa

Penguin Books Ltd, Registered Offices: 80 Strand, London WC2R ORL, England

www.penguin.com

Leon Trotsky Speaks first published in the USA by Pathfinder Press 1972
These extracts published in Penguin Books by kind permission of Pathfinder Press 2008

1

Copyright © Pathfinder Press, 1972
All rights reserved

Set by Rowland Phototypesetting Ltd, Bury St Edmunds, Suffolk
Printed in England by Clays Ltd, St Ives plc

978-0-141-04256-5

www.greenpenguin.co.uk

Penguin Books is committed to a sustainable future
for our business, our readers and our planet.
The book in your hands is made from paper
certified by the Forest Stewardship Council.

Contents

Planning Revolution

1. The Zimmerwald Manifesto Against the War

Drawn up by Trotsky in September 1915 following a revolutionary conference in Zimmerwald, Switzerland.

Proletarians of Europe!

The war has lasted more than a year. Millions of corpses cover the battlefields. Millions of human beings have been crippled for the rest of their lives. Europe is like a gigantic human slaughterhouse. All civilization, created by the labour of many generations, is doomed to destruction. The most savage barbarism is today celebrating its triumph over all that hitherto constituted the pride of mankind.

Irrespective of the truth as to the direct responsibility for the outbreak of the war, one thing is certain: the war that has produced this chaos is the outcome of imperialism, of the attempt on the part of the capitalist classes of each nation to foster their greed for profit by the exploitation of human labour and of the natural resources of the entire globe.

Economically backward or politically weak nations are thereby subjugated by the great powers who, in this war, are seeking to remake the world map with blood and iron in accord with their exploiting interests. Thus entire nations and countries like Belgium, Poland, the Balkan states, and Armenia are threatened with the fate of being torn asunder, annexed as a whole or in part as booty in the game of compensations.

In the course of the war, its driving forces are revealed in all their vileness. Shred after shred falls the veil with which the meaning of this world catastrophe was hidden from the consciousness of the people. The capitalists of all countries, who are coining the gold of war profits out of the blood shed by the people, assert that the war is for defence of the fatherland, for democracy, and the liberation of oppressed nations. They lie! In actual reality, they are burying the freedom of their own people together with the independence of the other nations on the fields of devastation. New fetters, new chains, new burdens are arising, and it is the proletariat of all countries, of the victorious as well as of the conquered countries, that will have to bear them. Improvement in welfare was proclaimed at the outbreak of the war – want and privation, unemployment and high prices, undernourishment and epidemics are the actual results. The burdens of war will consume the best energies of the peoples for decades, endanger the achievements of social reform, and hinder every step forward.

Cultural devastation, economic decline, political reaction – these are the blessings of this horrible conflict of nations.

Thus the war reveals the naked figure of modern capitalism which has become irreconcilable not only with the interests of the labouring masses, not only with the requirements of historical development, but also with the elementary conditions of human intercourse.

The ruling powers of capitalist society who held the fate of the nations in their hands, the monarchic as well as the republican governments, the secret diplomacy, the mighty business organizations, the bourgeois parties, the capitalist press, the church – all these bear the full weight of responsibility for this war which arose out of the social order fostering them and protected by them, and which is being waged for their interests.

Workers!

Exploited, disfranchised, scorned, they called you brothers and comrades at the outbreak of the war when you were to be led to the slaughter, to death. And now that militarism has crippled you, mutilated you, degraded and annihilated you, the rulers demand that you surrender your interests, your aims, your ideals – in a word, servile subordination to civil peace. They rob you of the possibility of expressing your views, your feelings, your pains; they prohibit you from raising your demands and defending them. The press gagged, political rights and liberties trod upon – this is the way the military dictatorship rules today with an iron hand.

This situation which threatens the entire future of Europe and of humanity cannot and must not be confronted by us any longer without action. The Socialist proletariat has waged a struggle against militarism for decades. With growing concern, its representatives at their national and international congresses occupied themselves with the ever more menacing danger of war growing out of imperialism. At Stuttgart, at Copenhagen, at Basle, the International Socialist congresses indicated the course which the proletariat must follow.

Since the beginning of the war Socialist parties and labour organizations of various countries that helped to determine this course have disregarded the obligations following from this. Their representatives have called upon the working class to give up the class struggle, the only possible and effective method of proletarian emancipation. They have granted credits to the ruling classes for waging the war; they have placed themselves at the disposal of the governments for the most diverse services; through their press and their messengers, they have tried to win the neutrals for the government policies of their countries; they have delivered up to their governments Socialist ministers as hostages for the preservation of civil peace, and thereby they have assumed the responsibility before the working class, before its present and its future, for this war, for its aims and its methods. And just as the individual parties, so the highest of the appointed representative bodies of the Socialists of all countries, the International Socialist Bureau has failed them.

These facts are equally responsible for the fact that the international working class, which did not succumb to the national panic of the first war period or which freed itself from it, has still, in the second year of the slaughter of peoples, found no ways and means of taking up an energetic struggle for peace simultaneously in all countries.

In this unbearable situation, we, the representatives of the Socialist parties, trade unions, or of their minorities, we Germans, French, Italians, Russians, Poles, Letts, Rumanians, Bulgarians, Swedes, Norwegians, Dutch, and Swiss, we who stand not on the ground of national solidarity with the exploiting class, but on the ground of the international solidarity of the proletariat and of the class struggle, have assembled to retie the torn threads of international relations and to call upon the working class to recover itself and to fight for peace.

This struggle is the struggle for freedom, for the reconciliation of peoples, for socialism. It is necessary to take up this struggle for peace, for a peace without annexations or war indemnities. Such a peace, however, is only possible if every thought of violating the rights and liberties of nations is condemned. Neither the occupation of entire countries nor of separate parts of countries must lead to their violent annexation. No annexation, whether open or concealed, and no forcible economic attachment made still more unbearable by political disfranchisement. The right of self-determination of nations must be the indestructible principle in the system of national relationships of peoples.

Proletarians!

Since the outbreak of the war you have placed your energy, your courage, your endurance at the service of the ruling classes. Now you must stand up for your own cause, for the sacred aims of socialism, for the emancipation of the oppressed nations as well as of the enslaved classes, by means of the irreconcilable proletarian class struggle.

It is the task and the duty of the Socialists of the belligerent countries to take up this struggle with full force; it is the task and the duty of the Socialists of the neutral states to support their brothers in this struggle against bloody barbarism with every effective means. Never in world history was there a more urgent, a more sublime task, the fulfilment of which should be our common labour. No sacrifice is too great, no burden too heavy in order to achieve this goal: peace among the people.

Workingmen and workingwomen! Mothers and fathers! Widows and orphans! Wounded and crippled! We call to all of you who are suffering from the war and because of the war: beyond all borders, beyond the reeking battlefields, beyond the devastated cities and villages –

Proletarians of all countries, unite!

2. *On the Eve of a Revolution*

This and the following three pieces, based on public speeches, were written for the New York-based Russian-language paper Novy Mir in March 1917 as Trotsky impatiently waited in New York for passports and visas to return to Russia.

The streets of Petrograd again speak the language of 1905. As in the time of the Russo-Japanese war, the masses demand bread, peace, and freedom. As in 1905, streetcars are not running and newspapers do not appear. The workingmen let the steam out of the boilers, they quit their benches, and walk out into the streets. The government mobilizes its Cossacks. And as in 1905, only those two powers are facing each other in the streets – the revolutionary workingmen and the army of the czar.

The movement was provoked by lack of bread. This, of course, is not an accidental cause. In all the belligerent countries the lack of bread is the most immediate, the most acute reason for dissatisfaction and indignation among the masses. All the insanity of the war is revealed to them from this angle: it is impossible to produce necessities of life because one has to produce instruments of death.

However, the attempts of the Anglo-Russian semi-official news agencies to explain the movement by a temporary shortage in food or by snowstorms that have delayed transportation are one of the most ludicrous applications of the policy of the ostrich. The workingmen would not stop the factories, the streetcars, the print-shops and walk into the streets to meet czarism face to face on account of snowstorms which temporarily hamper the arrival of foodstuffs.

People have a short memory. Many of our own ranks have forgotten that the war found Russia in a state of potent revolutionary ferment. After the heavy stupor of 1908–11, the proletariat gradually healed its wounds in the following years of industrial prosperity; the slaughter of strikers on the Lena river in April 1912 awakened the revolutionary energy of the proletarian masses. A series of strikes followed. In the year preceding the world war, the wave of economic and political strikes resembled that of 1905. When Poincaré, the president of the French republic, came to Petersburg in the summer of 1914 (evidently to talk over with the czar how to free the small and weak nations) the Russian proletariat was in a stage of extraordinary revolutionary tension, and the president of the French republic could see with his own eyes in the capital of his friend, the czar, how the first barricades of the second Russian revolution were being constructed.

The war checked the rising revolutionary tide. We have witnessed a repetition of what happened ten years before, in the Russo-Japanese war. After the stormy strikes of 1903, there had followed a year of almost unbroken political silence – 1904 – the first year of the war. It took the workingmen of Petersburg twelve months to orient themselves in the war and to walk out into the streets with their demands and protests. January 9, 1905, was, so to speak, the official beginning of our first revolution.

The present war is vaster than was the Russo-Japanese war. Millions of soldiers have been mobilized by the government for the 'defence of the fatherland'. The ranks of the proletariat have thus been disorganized. On the other hand, the more advanced elements of the proletariat had to face and weigh in their minds a number of questions of unheard-of magnitude. What is the cause of the war? Shall the proletariat agree with the conception of 'the defence of the fatherland'? What ought to be the tactics of the working class in wartime?

In the meantime, czarism and its allies, the upper groups of the nobility and the bourgeoisie, had during the war completely exposed their true nature – the nature of criminal plunderers, blinded by limitless greed and paralysed by want of talent. The appetites for conquest of the governing clique grew in proportion as the people began to realize its complete inability to cope with the most elementary problems of warfare, of industry and supplies in wartime. Simultaneously, the misery of the people grew, deepened, became more and more acute – a natural result of the war multiplied by the criminal anarchy of Rasputin czarism.

In the depths of the great masses, among people who may have never been reached by a word of propaganda, a profound bitterness accumulated under the stress of events. Meantime the foremost ranks of the proletariat were finishing digesting the new events. The Socialist proletariat of Russia came to after the shock of the nationalist fall of the most influential part of the International, and decided that new times call us not to let up, but to increase our revolutionary struggle.

The present events in Petrograd and Moscow are a result of this internal preparatory work.

A disorganized, compromised, disjointed government on top. An utterly demoralized army. Dissatisfaction, uncertainty, and fear among the propertied classes. At the bottom, among the masses, a deep bitterness. A proletariat numerically stronger than ever, hardened in the fire of events. All this warrants the statement that we are witnessing the beginning of the second Russian revolution. Let us hope that many of us will be its participants.

3. Two Faces – Internal Forces of the Russian Revolution

Let us examine more closely what is going on.

Nicholas has been dethroned and, according to some information, is under arrest. The most conspicuous Black Hundred leaders have been arrested. Some of the most hated have been killed. A new ministry has been formed consisting of Octobrists, liberals, and the radical Kerensky. A general amnesty has been proclaimed.

All these are facts, big facts. These are the facts that strike the outer world most. Changes in the higher government give the bourgeoisie of Europe and America an occasion to say that the revolution has won and is now completed.

The czar and his Black Hundred fought for their power, for this alone. The war, the imperialistic plans of the Russian bourgeoisie, the interests of the Allies were of minor importance to the czar and his clique. They were ready at any moment to conclude peace with the Hohenzollerns and Hapsburgs, to free their most loyal regiment for war against their own people.

The Progressive Bloc of the Duma mistrusted the czar and his ministers. This bloc consisted of various parties of the Russian bourgeoisie. The bloc had two aims: one, to conduct the war to a victorious end; another, to secure internal reforms – more order, control, accounting. A victory is necessary for the Russian bourgeoisie to conquer markets, to increase their territories, to get rich. Reforms are necessary primarily to enable the Russian bourgeoisie to win the war.

The progressive imperialistic bloc wanted *peaceful* reforms. The liberals intended to exert a Duma pressure on the monarchy and to keep it in check with the aid of the governments of Great Britain and France. They did not want a revolution. They knew that a revolution, bringing the working masses to the front, would be a menace to their domination, and primarily a menace to their imperialistic plans. The labouring masses, in the cities and in the villages, and even in the army itself, want peace. The liberals know it. This is why they have been enemies of the revolution all these years. A few months ago Miliukov declared in the Duma: 'If a revolution were necessary for victory, I would prefer no victory at all.'

Yet the liberals are now in power – through the revolution. The bourgeois newspapermen see nothing but this fact. Miliukov, already in his capacity as a minister of foreign affairs, has declared that the revolution has been conducted in the name of a victory over the enemy, and that the new government has taken upon itself to continue the war to a victorious end. The New York Stock Exchange interpreted the revolution in this specific sense. There are clever people both on the stock exchange and among the bourgeois newspapermen. Yet they are all amazingly stupid when they come to deal with mass movements. They think that Miliukov manages the revolution, in the same sense as they manage their banks or news offices. They see only the liberal governmental reflection of the unfolding events, they notice only the foam on the surface of the historical torrent.

The long pent-up dissatisfaction of the masses has burst forth so late, in the thirty-second month of the war, not because the masses were held by police barriers – those barriers had been badly shattered during the war – but because all liberal institutions and organs, together with their social-patriotic shadows, were exerting an enormous influence over the least enlightened elements of the workingmen, urging them to keep order and discipline in the name of 'patriotism'. Hungry women were already walking out into the streets, and the workingmen were getting ready to uphold them by a general strike, while the liberal bourgeoisie, according to news reports, still issued proclamations and delivered speeches to check the movement – resembling that famous heroine of Dickens who tried to stem the tide of the ocean with a broom.

The movement, however, took its course, from below, from the workingmen's quarters. After hours and days of uncertainty, of shooting, of skirmishes, the army joined in the revolution, from below, from the best of the soldier masses. The old government was powerless, paralysed, annihilated. The czar fled from the capital 'to the front'. The Black Hundred bureaucrats crept, like cockroaches, each into his corner.

Then, and only then, came the Duma's turn to act. The czar had attempted in the last minute to dissolve it. And the Duma would have obeyed, 'following the example of former years', had it been free to adjourn. The capitals, however, were already dominated by the revolutionary people, the same people that had walked out into the streets despite the wishes of the liberal bourgeoisie. The army was with the people. Had not the bourgeoisie attempted to organize its own government, a revolutionary government would have emerged from the revolutionary working masses. The Duma of June 3 would never have dared to seize the power from the hands of czarism. But it did not want to miss the chance offered by interregnum: the monarchy had disappeared, while a revolutionary government was not yet formed. Contrary to all their part, contrary to their own policies and against their will, the liberals found themselves in possession of power.

Miliukov now declares Russia will continue the war 'to the end'. It is not easy for him to speak so: he knows that his words are apt to arouse the indignation of the masses against the new government. Yet he had to speak them – for the sake of the London, Paris, and American stock exchanges. It is quite possible that he cabled his declaration for foreign consumption only, and that he concealed it from his own country.

Miliukov knows very well that *under given conditions he cannot continue the war, crush Germany, dismember Austria, occupy Constantinople and Poland.*

The masses have revolted, demanding bread and peace. The appearance of a few liberals at the head of the government has not fed the hungry, has not healed the wounds of the people. To satisfy the most urgent, the most acute needs of the people, *peace* must be restored. The liberal imperialistic bloc does not dare to speak of peace. They do not do it, first, on account of the Allies. They do not do it, further, because the liberal bourgeoisie is to a great extent responsible before the people for the

present war. The Miliukovs and Guchkovs, not less than
the Romanov camarilla, have thrown the country into
this monstrous imperialistic adventure. To stop the war,
to return to the antebellum misery would mean that
they have to account to the people for this under-
taking. The Miliukovs and Guchkovs are afraid of the
liquidation of the war not less than they were afraid of
the revolution.

This is their aspect in their new capacity, as the government of Russia. They are compelled to continue the war,
and they can have no hope of victory; they are afraid of
the people, and the people do not trust them.

This is how Karl Marx characterized a similar situation:

From the very beginning ready to betray the people and
to compromise with the crowned representatives of the old
regime, because the bourgeoisie itself belongs to the old world;
. . . keeping a place at the steering wheel of the revolution not
because the people were back of them, but because the people
pushed them forward; . . . having no faith in themselves, no
faith in the people; grumbling against those above, trembling
before those below; selfish towards both fronts and aware of
their selfishness; revolutionary in the face of conservatives, and
conservative in the face of revolutionists, with no confidence in
their own slogans and with phrases instead of ideas; frightened
by the world's storm and exploiting the world's storm – vulgar
through lack of originality, and original only in vulgarity;
making profitable business out of their own desires, with no
initiative, with no vocation for worldwide historic work . . . a
cursed senile creature condemned to direct and abuse in his
own senile interests the first youthful movements of a power-

ful people – a creature with no eyes, with no ears, with no teeth, with nothing whatever – this is how the Prussian bourgeoisie stood at the steering wheel of the Prussian state after the March revolution.

These words of the great master give a perfect picture of the Russian liberal bourgeoisie as it stands at the steering wheel of the government after *our* March revolution. 'With no faith in themselves, with no faith in the people, with no eyes, with no teeth.' . . . This is their political face.

Luckily for Russia and Europe, there is another face to the Russian revolution, a genuine face: the cables have brought the news that the Provisional Government is opposed by a Workmen's Committee which has already raised a voice of protest against the liberal attempt to rob the revolution and to deliver the people to the monarchy.

Should the Russian revolution stop today, as the representatives of liberalism advocate, tomorrow the reaction of the czar, the nobility, and the bureaucracy would gather power and drive Miliukov and Guchkov from their insecure ministerial trenches, as did the Prussian reaction years ago with the representatives of Prussian liberalism. But the Russian revolution will not stop. Time will come, and the revolution will make a clean sweep of the bourgeois liberals blocking its way, as it is now making a clean sweep of czarist reaction.

4. The Growing Conflict

An open conflict between the forces of the revolution, headed by the city proletariat, and the anti-revolutionary liberal bourgeoisie temporarily at the head of the government is more and more impending. It cannot be avoided. Of course, the liberal bourgeoisie and the quasi-socialists of the vulgar type will find a collection of very touching slogans as to 'national unity' against class divisions; yet no one has ever succeeded in removing social contrasts by conjuring with words or in checking the natural progress of revolutionary struggle.

The internal history of unfolding events is known to us only in fragments, through casual remarks in the official telegrams. But even now it is apparent that on two points the revolutionary proletariat is bound to oppose the liberal bourgeoisie with ever-growing determination.

The first conflict has already arisen around the question of the form of government. The Russian bourgeoisie needs a monarchy. In all the countries pursuing an imperialistic policy, we observe an unusual increase of personal power. The policy of world usurpations, secret treaties, and open treachery requires independence from parliamentary control and a guarantee against changes in policies caused by the change of cabinets. Moreover, for the propertied classes the monarchy is the most secure ally in its struggle against the revolutionary onslaught of the proletariat.

In Russia both these causes are more effective than elsewhere. The Russian bourgeoisie finds it impossible to deny the people universal suffrage, well aware that this would arouse opposition against the Provisional Government among the masses, and give prevalence to the left, the more determined wing of the proletariat in the revolution. Even that monarch of the reserve, Michael Alexandrovich, understands that he cannot reach the throne without having promised 'universal, equal, direct, and secret suffrage'. It is the more essential for the bourgeoisie to create right now a monarchic counterbalance against the deepest social revolutionary demands of the working masses. *Formally*, in words, the bourgeoisie has agreed to leave the question of a form of government to the discretion of the Constituent Assembly. Practically, however, the Octobrist-Cadet Provisional Government will turn all the preparatory work for the Constituent Assembly into a campaign in favour of a monarchy against a republic. The character of the Constituent Assembly will largely depend upon the character of those who convoke it. It is evident, therefore, that right now the revolutionary proletariat will have *to set up its own organs, the Councils of Working-men's, Soldiers', and Peasants' Deputies, against the executive organs of the Provisional Government*. In this struggle the proletariat ought to unite about itself the rising masses of the people, with one aim in view – *to seize governmental power*. Only a revolutionary labour government will have the desire and ability to give the country a thorough democratic cleansing during the work preparatory to the Constituent Assembly, to reconstruct the army from top to bottom, to turn it into *a revolutionary militia*, and to show the poorer peasants in practice that their only salvation is in support of a revolutionary labour regime. A Constituent Assembly convoked after such preparatory work will truly reflect the revolutionary, creative forces of the country and become a powerful factor in the further development of the revolution.

The second question that is bound to bring the internationally inclined Socialist proletariat in opposition to the imperialistic liberal bourgeoisie is *the question of war and peace*.

5. War or Peace?

The question of chief interest, now, to the governments and the peoples of the world is: What will be the influence of the Russian revolution on the war? Will it bring peace nearer? Or will the revolutionary enthusiasm of the people swing towards a more vigorous prosecution of the war?

This is a great question. On its solution depends not only the outcome of the war, but the fate of the revolution itself.

In 1905, Miliukov, the present militant minister of foreign affairs, called the Russo-Japanese war an adventure and demanded its immediate cessation. This was also the spirit of the liberal and radical press. The strongest industrial organizations favoured immediate peace in spite of unequalled disasters. Why was it so? Because they expected internal reforms. The establishment of a constitutional system, a parliamentary control over the budget and the state finances, a better school system and, especially, an increase in the land possessions of the peasants would, they hoped, increase the prosperity of the population and create a *vast internal market* for Russian industry. It is true that even then, twelve years ago, the Russian bourgeoisie was ready to usurp land belonging to others. It hoped, however, that abolition of feudal relations in the village would create a more powerful market than the annexation of Manchuria or Korea.

The democratization of the country and liberation of the peasants, however, turned out to be a slow process. Neither the czar, nor the nobility, nor the bureaucracy were willing to yield any of their prerogatives. Liberal exhortations were not enough to make them give up the machinery of the state and their land possessions. A revolutionary onslaught of the masses was required. This the bourgeoisie did not want. The agrarian revolts of the peasants, the ever-growing struggle of the proletariat, and the spread of insurrections in the army caused the liberal bourgeoisie to fall back into the camp of the czarist bureaucracy and reactionary nobility. Their alliance was sealed by the coup d'etat of June 3, 1907. Out of this coup d'etat emerged the Third and the Fourth Dumas.

The peasants received no land. The administrative system changed only in name, not in substance. The development of an internal market consisting of prosperous farmers, after the American fashion, did not take place. The capitalist classes, reconciled with the regime of June 3, turned their attention to the usurpation of foreign markets. A new era of Russian imperialism ensues, an imperialism accompanied by a disorderly financial and military system and by insatiable appetites. Guchkov, the present war minister, was formerly a member of the Committee on National Defence, helping to make the army and the navy complete. Miliukov, the present minister of foreign affairs, worked out a programme of world conquests which he advocated on his trips to Europe. Russian imperialism and its Octobrist and Cadet representatives bear a great part of the responsibility for the present war.

By the grace of the revolution which they had not wanted and which they had fought, Guchkov and Miliukov are now in power. For the continuation of the war, for victory? Of course! They are the same persons who had dragged the country into the war for the sake of the interests of capital. All their opposition to czarism had its source in their unsatisfied imperialistic appetites. So long as the clique of Nicholas II was in power, the interests of the dynasty and of the reactionary nobility were prevailing in Russian foreign affairs. This is why Berlin and Vienna had hoped to conclude a separate peace with Russia. Now, purely imperialistic interests have superseded the czarist interests; pure imperialism is written on the banner of the Provisional Government. 'The government of the czar is gone,' the Miliukovs and Guchkovs say to the people, 'now you must shed your blood for the common interests of the entire nation.' Those interests the imperialists understand as the reincorporation of Poland, the conquest of Galicia, Constantinople, Armenia, Persia.

This transition from an imperialism of the dynasty and the nobility to an imperialism of a purely bourgeois character can never reconcile the Russian proletariat to the war. An international struggle against the world slaughter and imperialism are now our task more than ever. The last dispatches which tell of anti-militaristic propaganda in the streets of Petrograd show that our comrades are bravely doing their duty.

The imperialistic boasts of Miliukov to crush Germany, Austria, and Turkey are the most effective and most timely aid for the Hohenzollerns and Hapsburgs . . . Miliukov will now serve as a scarecrow in their hands. The liberal imperialistic government of Russia has not yet started reform in its own army, yet it is already helping the Hohenzollerns to raise the patriotic spirit and to mend the shattered 'national unity' of the German people. Should the German proletariat be given a right to think that all the Russian people and the main force of the Russian revolution, the proletariat, are behind the bourgeois government of Russia, it would be a terrific blow to the men of our trend of mind, the revolutionary socialists of Germany. To turn the Russian proletariat into patriotic cannon fodder in the service of the Russian liberal bourgeoisie would mean *to throw the German working masses into the camp of the chauvinists and for a long time to halt the progress of a revolution in Germany.*

The prime duty of the revolutionary proletariat in Russia is to show that there is *no power* behind the evil imperialistic will of the liberal bourgeoisie. The Russian revolution has to show the entire world its real face.

The further progress of the revolutionary struggle in Russia and the creation of a revolutionary labour government supported by the people will be a mortal blow to the Hohenzollerns because it will give a powerful stimulus to the revolutionary movement of the German proletariat and of the labour masses of all the other countries. If the first Russian revolution of 1905 brought about revolutions in Asia – in Persia, Turkey, China – the second Russian revolution will be the beginning of a powerful social revolutionary struggle in Europe. Only this struggle will bring real peace to the blood-drenched world.

No, the Russian proletariat will not allow itself to be harnessed to the chariot of Miliukov imperialism. The banner of Russian Social Democracy is now, more than ever before, glowing with bright slogans of inflexible internationalism:

Away with imperialistic robbers!

Long live a revolutionary labour government!

Long live peace and the brotherhood of nations!

6. All Power to the Soviets

On arrival in Petrograd, Trotsky gave a major speech on May 5 to the Petrograd Soviet, aligning himself with the left wing. This is probably a summary rather than the exact text.

News of the Russian Revolution found us in New York but even in that great country, where the bourgeoisie dominates as nowhere else, the Russian Revolution has done its work. The American labourer has had some unfavourable things said about him. It is said that he does not support the revolution. But had you seen the American workman in February, you would have been doubly proud of your revolution. You would have understood that it has shaken not only Russia, not only Europe, but America. It would have been clear to you, as to me, that it has opened a new epoch, an epoch of blood and iron, not in a war of nations, but in a war of the oppressed classes against the domineering classes. [*Tumultuous applause.*] At all the meetings, the workers asked me to give you their warmest greetings. [*Applause.*] But I must tell you something about the Germans. I had an opportunity to come in close contact with a group of German proletarians. You ask me where? In a prisoner-of-war camp. The bourgeois English government arrested us as enemies and placed us in a prisoner-of-war camp in Canada. [*Cries: 'Shame!'*] About one hundred German officers and eight hundred sailors were there. They asked me how it happened that we, Russian citizens, became prisoners of the English. When I told them that we were prisoners not because we were Russians, but because we were socialists, they said that they were slaves of their government, of their William. We got very close together with the German proletarians . . .

This talk did not please the German officers, and they made a complaint to the English commander that we were undermining the loyalty of the sailors to the kaiser. The English captain, anxious to preserve the allegiance of the German sailors to the kaiser, forbade me to lecture to them. The sailors protested to the commander. When we departed, the sailors accompanied us with music and shouted, 'Down with William! Down with the bourgeoisie! Long live the united international proletariat!'

[*Great applause.*] That which passed through the brains of the German sailors is passing through in all countries. The Russian Revolution is the prologue to the world revolution.

But I cannot conceal that I do not agree with everything. I regard it as dangerous to join the ministry. I do not believe that the ministry can perform miracles. We had, before, a dual government, due to the opposing points of view of two classes. The coalition government will not remove opposition, but will merely transfer it to the ministry. But the revolution will not perish because of the coalition government. We should, however, keep three precepts in mind: 1. Trust not the bourgeoisie. 2. Control our own leaders. 3. Have confidence in our own revolutionary strength.

What do we recommend? I think that the next step should be the handing over of all power to the Soviet of Workers' and Soldiers' Deputies. Only with the authority in one hand can Russia be saved. Long live the Russian Revolution as the prologue to the world revolution. [*Applause.*]

7. *In Answer to a Rumour*

As the Bolsheviks prepared to seize power from the Provisional Government, Trotsky gave this speech (reported here by a newspaper) on October 18.

During the last days the press has been full of communications, rumours, and articles about an impending

24

'action'; sometimes this action is attributed to the Bolsheviks, sometimes to the Petrograd Soviet.

The decisions of the Petrograd Soviet are published and made known to everybody. The Soviet is an elective institution; each of its members is responsible to the workers or soldiers who elected him. This revolutionary parliament of the proletariat and the revolutionary garrison cannot make a decision which is not known to the workers and soldiers.

We hide nothing. I declare in the name of the Soviet that no armed action has been settled upon by us, but if the Soviet in the course of events should be obliged to set the date for an action the workers and soldiers would come out to the last man at its summons.

The bourgeois press has set the day of the action for October 22. All the papers have repeated this 'subtle' prophecy. But October 22 has been unanimously arranged by the Executive Committee as a day of agitation, of propaganda, of bringing out the masses under the banner of the Soviet, and as a collection day on behalf of the Soviet.

Further, they say that I signed an order for five thousand rifles from the Sestroretsk factory. Yes, I signed it – by virtue of the decision already taken in the Kornilov days concerning the arming of the workers' militia. And the Petrograd Soviet will continue to organize and arm the workers' guard.

But all this news, all these 'facts' are surpassed by the newspaper *Den* [*The Day*].

Comrade Trotsky reads from yesterday's issue of *Den* the 'plan' of the Bolshevik action. This plan outlines the route to be followed by the Bolshevik 'armies' on the following night and indicates the places to be occupied. Nor was it forgotten to point out that the insurgents were to bring with them 'hooligan elements' from Novaya Derevnya. [*Laughter in the hall during the reading.*]

I beg you to listen carefully so that each army will know the route it has to follow! . . . [*Laughter.*]

Comrades – this news needs no comment just as the newspaper which published it needs no description.

The plan of the campaign is clear.

We are in conflict with the government on a question which may become extremely sharp. It is on the question of the evacuation of the troops. The bourgeois press wants to build up round the Petrograd workers an atmosphere of hostility and suspicion, and to provoke the hatred of the soldiers at the front for Petrograd.

Another sharp question is that of the Soviet Congress. The government circles know our views on the fundamental role of the Soviet Congress. It is known to the bourgeoisie that the Petrograd Soviet is going to propose to the Congress of Soviets that they take the power, offer a democratic peace to the belligerent peoples, and give the land to the peasants. So they are trying to disarm Petrograd by evacuating its garrison; and while the congress is arming itself, they arm those who obey them in order to be able to throw all their forces against the representatives of the workers, soldiers, and peasants, and break them up.

As an artillery barrage precedes an army's attack, the present campaign of lies and calumnies precedes an armed attack on the Soviet Congress.

We must be prepared. We are entering a period of bitter struggles. We must always expect an attack from the counter-revolution.

But at its first attempt to break up the Soviet Congress, at the first attempt at an attack, we shall answer with a counter-attack which will be ruthless and which we shall carry through to the end.

8. *Three Resolutions*

As the Bolshevik revolution approached, Trotsky drew up these Three Resolutions *on behalf of the Petrograd garrison's military committees. This is followed by Trotsky's appeal to Cossack troops not to hold a rumoured demonstration to clash with Petrograd Soviet Day on October 22.*

I. ON THE MILITARY REVOLUTIONARY COMMITTEE

Welcoming the setting up of a Military Revolutionary Committee attached to the Petrograd Soviet of Workers' and Soldiers' Deputies, the garrison of Petrograd and its environs promises the Military Revolutionary Committee full support in all its steps to link closely the front and the rear in the interests of the revolution.

2. OCTOBER 22 DAY

The garrison of Petrograd and its environs declares:

October 22 is to be a day devoted to a peaceful review of the forces of the Petrograd soldiers and workers and of collecting funds for the revolutionary press.

The garrison appeals to the Cossacks: BEWARE OF PROVOCATION BY OUR COMMON ENEMIES. We are your brothers. Together let us struggle for peace and freedom.

We invite you to our meetings tomorrow. You are welcome, brother Cossacks!

The Petrograd garrison also declares:

The entire garrison together with the organized proletariat assumes the maintenance of revolutionary order in Petrograd. Any provocative act by the Kornilovists and the bourgeoisie to bring disturbance and disorder into the revolutionary ranks will meet with A RUTHLESS COUNTERBLOW.

3. THE ALL-RUSSIAN CONGRESS OF SOVIETS OF WORKERS' AND SOLDIERS' DEPUTIES

Endorsing all the political decisions of the Petrograd Soviet of Workers' and Soldiers' Deputies, the Petrograd garrison declares:

THE TIME FOR WORDS HAS PASSED. The country is on the edge of ruin. The army demands peace, the peasants demand land, the workers demand work and food. The coalition government is against the people. It is a tool in the hands of the enemies of the people. The time for words has passed. The All-Russian Congress of Soviets must take the power and give the people peace, land, and food. The safety of the revolution and the people demands it.

ALL POWER TO THE SOVIETS!

IMMEDIATE ARMISTICE ON ALL FRONTS!

LAND TO THE PEASANTS!

HONEST SUMMONING OF THE CONSTITUENT ASSEMBLY AT THE APPOINTED DATE!

The Petrograd garrison solemnly promises the All-Russian Congress to give all the forces it can, to the last man, in the struggle for these demands.

Rely upon us, authorized representatives of the soldiers, workers, and peasants. We are all at our posts, READY TO CONQUER OR DIE!

9. *Brother Cossacks!*

Brother Cossacks!

The Petrograd Soviet of Soldiers' and Workers' Deputies appeals to you.

You, Cossacks, are being roused against us, workers and soldiers. It is our common foes who are carrying out this work of Cain: the oppressors of the court, the bankers, landlords, senior officials, former czarist servants. They have always been strong and powerful by dividing the people. They have poisoned the minds of the soldiers against the workers and peasants. They have set the Cossacks on the soldiers. By what means do they achieve this? By lies and slander. The Cossacks, soldiers, sailors, workers, and peasants are brothers. They are all toilers, all poor, they all work hard, they are all oppressed and robbed by the war.

Who's the war good for? Who started it? Not the Cossacks and not the soldiers, not the workers and not the peasants. It's the generals, bankers, czars, and landlords who need the war. They increase their power, their strength, their wealth, by war. They turn the people's blood into their masters' gold.

The people want peace. In all countries the soldiers and workers are thirsting for peace. The Petrograd Soviet of Workers' and Soldiers' Deputies says to the bourgeoisie and the generals: 'Move over, tyrants! Let power pass into the hands of the people themselves, and then the people will immediately conclude an honourable peace!'

Is that right, Comrade Cossacks? We do not doubt that you will say: Right! But that's the reason we are hated by all the usurers, the rich, the princes, the courtiers, and the generals, including your Cossack generals. They are ready at any hour to annihilate the Petrograd Soviet, to crush the revolution, and put back the shackles on the people as in the czar's time.

That's why they're telling you slanders about us. They are deceiving you. They say the Soviets want to take away your land. Don't believe them, Cossacks! The Soviet wants to take the land away from all the landowners and hand it over to the peasants, the corngrowers and also the poor Cossacks. Whose hand is raised to take the land away from the worker Cossack?

They tell you the Soviet is intending to make some sort of insurrection on October 22, to fight with you, shoot on the streets, kill. Those who told you that are rogues and provocateurs. Tell them so! On October 22 the Soviet has arranged peaceful meetings, assemblies, and concerts, where the workers and soldiers, sailors and peasants will hear and discuss speeches about war and peace, about the people's lot. We invite you too to these peaceful, fraternal meetings. You are welcome, brother Cossacks!

If any of you doubt this, come along to the Smolny, where the Soviet is. There are always many soldiers there, and Cossacks too. They will explain to the doubters what the Soviet wants, what are its aims and methods. That's what the people overthrew the czar for, to freely discuss their needs and take their affairs into their own hands. Cossacks, throw off the veil that the Kaledins, Bardizhes, Karaulovs and other enemies of the working Cossacks are pulling over your eyes.

Someone has arranged a Cossack religious procession for October 22. It is a matter for the free conscience of each Cossack whether or not to participate in the procession. We shall not interfere in this matter and will cause no trouble to anybody.

However, we warn you, Cossacks: be careful lest under the mask of a religious procession your Kaledins try to incite you against the workers and soldiers. Their goal is to bring about a bloodbath and to drown you and your liberty in brothers' blood.

Be assured: October 22 is Petrograd Soviet Day, a day of peaceful meetings, assemblies, and money collections for soldiers' and workers' newspapers. Join us, Cossacks – join the common family of the working people, for the common fight for freedom and happiness.

We stretch out a brotherly hand to you, Cossacks!

The Petrograd Soviet of
Workers' and Soldiers' Deputies

In Power

10. The Overthrow of the Provisional Government

Trotsky announces the fall of the government to the Petrograd Soviet on the afternoon of October 25.

In the name of the Military Revolutionary Committee, I declare the Provisional Government is no more. [*Applause.*] Some ministers have been arrested. [*Hurrahs!*] The others will be arrested in a few days or a few hours. [*Applause.*]

The revolutionary garrison, which is at the disposal of the Military Revolutionary Committee, has dissolved the meeting of the pre-Parliament. [*Stormy applause. Cries of 'Long live the Military Revolutionary Committee!'*]

They have told us that an insurrection of the garrison at the present moment would provoke a pogrom and drown the revolution in torrents of blood. Up till now no blood has flowed. We do not know of a single casualty. I do not know of any other example in history of a revolutionary movement involving such gigantic masses that was carried through without bloodshed.

The authority of the Provisional Government, presided over by Kerensky, was a corpse and only awaited the broom of history to sweep it away.

We must underline the heroism and self-sacrifice of

the Petrograd soldiers and workers. We have been awake here all night, and at the telephone followed how the detachments of revolutionary soldiers' and workers' guards went about their business quietly. The populace slept peacefully and did not know that at this very time one authority was replacing another.

The railway stations, post offices, telegraph stations, the Petrograd Telephone Agency, the State Bank have been occupied. [*Stormy applause.*]

The Winter Palace is not yet taken, but its fate will be settled in the course of the next few minutes. [*Applause.*]

The Petrograd Soviet of Workers' and Soldiers' Deputies has the right to be proud of the soldiers and workers on whom it relied, whom it led into battle and led to a glorious victory.

The characteristic of bourgeois and petty-bourgeois governments is to deceive the masses.

We, today, we, the Soviet of Soldiers', Workers', and Peasants' Deputies, are going to undertake an experiment unique in history, the establishment of a government that will have no other aim than the satisfaction of the needs of the soldiers, workers, and peasants.

The state must become the instrument of the masses in the struggle for their liberation from all slavery.

The work cannot be done without the influence of the Soviets. The best representatives of bourgeois science will understand that the conditions created by the Soviets of Workers', Soldiers', and Peasants' Deputies are the best for their work.

It is necessary to establish control over production.

Peasants, workers, and soldiers must feel that the nation's business is their business.

That is the fundamental principle of the establishment of the authority.

The introduction of universal labour service was one of the immediate tasks of genuine revolutionary power.

Further, Comrade Trotsky announced that on the agenda were the report of the Military Revolutionary Committee and the report on the tasks of Soviet power. The reporter on the second question would be Comrade Lenin. [*Thunderous applause.*]

Comrade Trotsky announced that those who had been arrested for political reasons had been released and some of them were already carrying out the duties of revolutionary commissars.

Comrade Zinoviev, announced Comrade Trotsky, would be the guest of the Petrograd Soviet in the current session.

In the name of the Petrograd Soviet a telegram had been circulated that night throughout the whole of Russia giving the real state of affairs.

Radiotelegrams had been sent to the forces on active service announcing the fall of the old authority and the imminent establishment of a new one. The first steps of the new authority would require the following: immediate armistice on all fronts; land to the peasants; urgent convocation of a genuinely democratic Constituent Assembly.

The whereabouts of the former minister-president Kerensky are unknown, but we hope it will soon become known to all.

To the question of what the attitude of the front was to the events, Comrade Trotsky replied: We have only been able to send our telegrams. No replies have been received to them, but we have heard here many times the representatives from the front rebuking us for not having taken vigorous steps.

Vladimir Ilyich Lenin has just come in and joined us; because of the course of circumstances he has not been able to come among us until now. Comrade Trotsky describes the role of Comrade Lenin in the history of the revolutionary movement in Russia, and proclaims:

Long live Comrade Lenin who has returned to us!

[Later in the same October 25 session, Trotsky answered an objection from the floor that the Bolsheviks were predetermining the will of the Second Congress.]

One of the immediate tasks of the Military Revolutionary Committee is to send delegations to tell the front about the revolution that has taken place in Petrograd.

The Petrograd Soviet must select from its midst commissars to be sent to the front. The Military Revolutionary Committee and its members cannot at the moment make reports since they are continuously taken up with urgent work. I can tell you that a telegram has just been received that troops from the front are moving in the direction of Petrograd. It is necessary to send revolutionary commissars over the whole country to tell the broad masses of the people what has happened.

[*A voice: 'You are predetermining the will of the All-Russian Congress of Soviets.'*]

The will of the All-Russian Congress of Soviets is

predetermined by the great fact of the insurrection of the workers and soldiers of Petrograd, which has taken place this night. Now we have only to consolidate our victory.

11. *The Walkout of the Mensheviks and Social Revolutionaries*

At the meeting of the Second All-Russian Congress of Soviets on the night of October 25 the Mensheviks and Social Revolutionaries walked out, consigning themselves, according to Trotsky, to 'the dustbin of history'. Trotsky, on behalf of the Bolsheviks, introduced the following resolution.

The Second All-Russian Congress of Soviets declares:

The walkout of the Menshevik and SR delegates from the congress is a completely impotent attempt to wreck the plenipotentiary representation of the worker and soldier masses at the very moment when the vanguard of these masses, with weapons in hand, is defending the congress and the revolution against counter-revolutionary attack.

The compromising parties by their past policies have caused incalculable losses to the cause of the revolution and have irreparably compromised themselves in the eyes of the workers, peasants, and soldiers.

The Compromisers prepared and approved the fatal offensive of June 18 which brought the army and the country to the edge of destruction.

The Compromisers supported the government of

capital punishment and treason to the people. For seven months the Compromisers supported the policy of systematic deception of the peasants on the land question.

The Compromisers supported the suppression of revolutionary organizations, the disarming of the workers, the introduction of Kornilovist discipline into the army and the purposeless dragging out of the bloody war.

The Compromisers in fact helped their bourgeois allies deepen the economic ruin in the land, condemning millions of the toiling masses to famine.

Having lost the confidence of the masses as a result of this policy, the Compromisers, artificially and dishonestly, kept for themselves top positions in the Soviet and army organizations which for a long time had not been up for re-election.

In view of the stated circumstances, the Central Executive Committee has made every effort to wreck the Congress of Soviets, relying for that on the compromising army committees and on the direct support of the government authority.

When this policy of obstructing and falsifying the revolutionary class's public opinion suffered a lamentable failure; when the Provisional Government, set up by the Compromisers, fell under the blows of the Petrograd workers and soldiers; when the All-Russian Congress of Soviets showed clearly the predominance of the party of revolutionary socialism; and when insurrection became the only way out for the revolutionary masses, deceived and tormented by the bourgeoisie and their lackeys, then the Compromisers drew the final conclusions for themselves, and broke with the Soviets whose power they had tried vainly to undermine.

The walkout of the Compromisers does not weaken the Soviets but strengthens them as it cleanses the workers' and peasants' revolution of counter-revolutionary ingredients.

Having heard the statements of the SRs and the Mensheviks, the Second All-Russian Congress continues its work whose aims are determined by the will of the toiling people and its insurrection of October 24–25.

Down with the Compromisers! Down with the lackeys of the bourgeoisie! Long live the victorious insurrection of the soldiers, workers, and peasants!

12. *On the Arrest of Socialist Ministers*

Trotsky's response to a query the following day at the Second Congress about the fate of the Menshevik and Social Revolutionary ministers.

Here two questions are being confused, comrades. One of them was settled by us yesterday in businesslike fashion. It was decided that the Socialist ministers, Mensheviks and SRs, should be temporarily placed under house arrest by the Military Revolutionary Committee. That is what happened to Prokopovich; that's what we are going to do to Maslov and Salazkin. The Military Revolutionary Committee is taking every measure to carry out your decisions to the full, in the shortest possible time; and if it has not been done yet it is because, comrades, we are passing through an armed insurrection when another representative of one of these parties, Kerensky – who is well known to us – is organizing counter-revolutionary forces to hurl against us. Occupied till now with saving the victorious workers' and peasants' revolution, the Military Revolutionary Committee neglected two Socialist ministers in order that the workers' and peasants' revolution would not suffer harm. [*Applause.*]

The second question is that of the impression made on the public by these arrests. Comrades, we are passing through new times when the usual ideas must be discarded. Our revolution is the victory of new classes who have come to power and who must defend themselves against the organization of counter-revolutionary forces in which the Socialist ministers participated. But they are only subjected to house arrest until their participation in the organization of the counter-revolutionary conspiracy is established. By themselves, these two ministers do not represent any danger to us, either morally, politically, or in the slightest significant way.

We are told that nothing like this has happened in any other revolution. Those who say so have short memories, because this very thing happened a few months ago when members of the Executive Committee of Workers' and Soldiers' Deputies were arrested with the full connivance and agreement of these same Socialist ministers, and there was no protest, no demand for their liberation. That is not all: no other than the chairman of the Executive Committee of the Peasants'

Deputies, Avksentiev, posted two men from the Okhrana at the doors of Alexandra Mikhailovna Kollontai's flat though she had been set free by the magistrates. Now these same representatives come to tear us away from official work, trouble us in the middle of most serious matters in which they can take no part, in order to shout into our ears their impotent threats and lay before us their tearful indignation. [*Loud applause.*]

13. *The Organization of Power*

In further debates at the Second Congress, Trotsky responded to the proposal that all Congress parties should be included in government, even if they had walked out.

The considerations we have heard here have been brought against us more than once. They have tried to frighten us again and again with the possible isolation of the left wing. A few days ago when the question of an insurrection was openly raised, we were told we were isolating ourselves, we were heading for destruction, and in fact, if one were to judge from the political press what the class groupings were, then an insurrection threatened us with inevitable ruin.

Against us were counter-revolutionary bands and defencists of all varieties. One wing of the Left SRs worked courageously with us in the Military Revolutionary Committee. The rest of them took up a position of watchful neutrality. Nevertheless, even under these unfavourable conditions, when it seemed we were abandoned by everybody, the insurrection triumphed, almost without bloodshed.

If we had really been isolated, if the real forces had genuinely been against us, how could it have come about that we gained a victory almost without bloodshed? No, it was not we who were isolated, but the government and the democrats – the pseudo-democrats. It was they who were isolated from the masses. By their wavering, their compromising, they cut themselves off from the ranks of the real democracy.

Our great advantage as a party lies in the fact that we have formed a coalition with the masses, creating a coalition of the workers, soldiers, and poorest peasants.

Political groupings disappear, but the basic interests of classes remain. The party which prevails is the one that is able to understand and to satisfy the basic demands of classes. If a coalition was necessary then that coalition is the coalition of our garrison, chiefly composed of peasants, with the working class. We can be proud of such a coalition. This coalition has been tested in the fire of struggle. The Petrograd garrison and proletariat, as one, entered into the great struggle which will be the classic example of revolution in the history of all peoples.

We have been told here about the Left Bloc set up in the pre-Parliament, but this bloc lasted only one day; evidently it had not been formed in the place where it should have been. Perhaps both the bloc and programme were good; nevertheless one collision was sufficient for the bloc to crumble into dust.

Comrade Avilov has spoken of the great difficulties with which we are faced. To remove all these difficulties he proposes the formation of a coalition. But in this he makes no attempt to clarify this formula, to define more accurately what kind of coalition he has in mind. A coalition of groups, or classes, or simply a coalition of newspapers? For, after all, before talking of a coalition, for example, with the old Central Executive Committee, you have to understand that a coalition with the Dans and the Liebers would not strengthen the revolution but would serve as a reason for its ruin. At the most critical moment of the struggle we were left without a telephone, with the connivance of the CEC commissars.

They say that the split in the democracy is a misunderstanding. When Kerensky sends shock troops against us, when they deal us blow after blow, can one really talk of a misunderstanding? If this is a misunderstanding, I am afraid that all the arguments of our opponents – Comrades Avilov and Karelin – are also a political misunderstanding.

Comrade Avilov has told us: There is not much bread; we must have a coalition with the defencists. But will this coalition really increase the quantity of bread? The whole question of bread is a question of the programme of action. The struggle against economic collapse demands a definite system of action and not merely political groupings.

Comrade Avilov talked about the peasantry. But again, what peasantry is one talking about? We must choose between the different elements of the peasantry. Today, and right here, a representative of the peasants of Tver province demanded the arrest of Avksentiev. We must choose between the Tver peasant who demands the arrest of Avksentiev, and Avksentiev who has filled the prisons with members of the peasant committees. We are with the Tver peasants against Avksentiev. We are with them to the end and indissolubly. We firmly reject coalition with the kulak elements of the peasantry in the name of coalition of the working class and the poorest peasants.

If the revolution has taught us anything then it is this – that it is only by way of agreement, by way of a genuine coalition of these elements, that victory can be achieved. Those who chase the shadow of coalition are isolating themselves from life. The Left SRs will lose support among the masses to the extent that they venture to oppose themselves to our party; a party which opposes itself to the party of the proletariat, with whom the village poor have united, isolates itself from the revolution.

Openly and in front of the whole people we raised the banner of insurrection. The political formula of this insurrection was: All power to the Soviets – through the Congress of Soviets. We are told: You did not wait for the congress. No, we would have waited for it but Kerensky did not want to wait; the counter-revolutionaries were not sleeping. We as a party considered it our task to create a real chance for the Congress of Soviets to take power into its hands. If the congress had been surrounded by junkers how could it have taken the power into its hands? To achieve this task, what was needed was a party which would wrest the power from the hands of the counter-revolutionaries and say to you: 'Here is the power and you are obliged to take it!' [*Stormy, continuous applause.*]

Despite the fact that the defencists of all shades stopped at nothing in their struggle against us, we did not reject them. We proposed to the congress as a whole to take the power into its hands. How utterly you distort the perspective when you talk about our irreconcilability. How, after all that has happened, is it possible to speak of our irreconcilability? When a party surrounded by a cloud of gunpowder smoke comes to them and says, 'Let us take the power together!' they run to the city Duma and there unite with open counter-revolutionaries! They are traitors to the revolution with whom we will never unite!

For a successful struggle for peace, said Comrade Avilov, we must have a coalition with the Compromisers. At the same time he said that the Allies do not want to conclude peace; but if we rally to those who are betraying us everything will be fine. The Allied imperialists laughed, says Avilov, at the margarine democrat Skobelev. But nevertheless he advised us: If you form a bloc with the margarine democrats, the cause of peace will be assured!

There are two ways in the struggle for peace. One way is to oppose to the Allied and enemy governments the moral and material forces of the revolution. The other way is a bloc with Skobelev, which means a bloc with Tereshchenko, that is, complete submission to Allied imperialism.

It is pointed out to us that in our proclamation on peace we address ourselves at the same time to the governments and the peoples. This is only a formal equality.

We of course are not thinking of influencing the imperialist governments with our proclamations; but as long as they exist we cannot ignore them. But we rest all our hope on the unleashing of the European revolution by our revolution. If the insurrectionary peoples of Europe do not crush imperialism, we will be crushed – that is beyond doubt. Either the Russian Revolution will raise the whirlwind of struggle in the West or the capitalists of all countries will crush our revolution.

[*'There is a third way,' says someone from his seat.*]

The third way is the way of the Central Executive Committee – which on the one hand has sent delegations to the West European workers and on the other has formed an alliance with the Kishkins and Konovalovs. That is the way of lies and hypocrisy which we will never take.

Of course, we do not say that the first day of the insurrection of the European workers will inevitably be the day of the signing of the peace treaty. It is also possible that the bourgeoisie, frightened by the approaching insurrection of all the oppressed, will hasten to conclude peace. The dates are not set. No concrete forms can be foreseen. It is important and necessary to determine the method of struggle, which in principle is identical in both foreign and domestic policies. The alliance of the oppressed, always and everywhere – that is our way.

The Second Congress of Soviets has elaborated a whole programme of measures. Any group that wishes to realize this programme in fact, which at this critical moment takes its place on this side of the barricade, will meet with only one statement from us: 'Welcome, dear comrades, we are brothers-in-arms and we shall go with you to the end.'

[*Stormy and prolonged applause.*]

14. For Peace – Against Secret Diplomacy!

On November 21 Trotsky gave this speech as commissar of foreign affairs to an audience of some 12,000 at the Modern Circus in Petrograd.

In this building on October 23 I spoke to a popular meeting at which the question of an All-Russian Congress was being discussed, and all voices were raised in favour of Soviet power. The question which had been most emphatically before the people in all the eight months of the revolution was the question of war and peace, and we maintained that only a power basing its authority directly on the people could put an end to the slaughter. We maintained that the secret treaties must be published, and declared that the Russian people, not having made these treaties, could not be bound to carry out the conquests agreed upon therein. Our enemies answered that this was demagogy. You would never dare if you were in power, they said, to do this, for then the Allies would oppose us. But we maintained that the salvation of Russia was in peace. We pointed out that the prolonged character of the war was destroying the revolution, was exhausting and destroying the country, and that the longer we should fight the more complete the slavish position we should then occupy, so that at last we should merely be left the choice of picking a master.

We desire to live and develop as a free nation; but for the conclusion of peace, we had to overthrow the power of the bourgeoisie and of Kerensky. They told us we would be left without any supporters. But on October 25 the local Soviet of Petrograd took the initiative upon itself as well as the responsibility and, with the aid of the garrison and the workers, accomplished the insurrection and appeared before the Congress of Soviets then in session and said: 'The old power in the country is broken, there is no authority anywhere, and we are obliged to take it into our own hands.' We have said that the first obligation devolving upon the new power is the offering of peace parleys on all fronts, for the conclusion of a peace without annexations or indemnities on the basis of self-determination of peoples, that is, each people, through popular elections, must speak for itself the decisive word: Do they wish to enter into a confederation with their present sovereign state, enjoying full autonomy under it, or do they wish to separate themselves from it and have full independence? We must put a stop to a condition in which the strong can by force of arms compel the weak to assume what conditions of life the strong may desire: every people, be it great or small, must be the master of its own fate. Now this is the programme not of a party, not of a Soviet, but of the whole people, excepting the predatory party which dares call itself the Party of Popular Liberty but which in reality is an enemy of popular liberty, fighting against peace with all its might, and against which we have declared our implacable hostility – with the exception of this party, the whole Russian people has declared that it will not tolerate the use of force. And this is the spirit in which we issue our peace decree.

On the day on which we passed this decree Krasnov's Cossacks rebelled and danger threatened the very existence of the Soviet power. Yet hardly had they been defeated and the Soviet authority strengthened, when our first act was to turn to the Allied and German authorities, simultaneously, with a proposition for peace parleys on all fronts. Our enemies, the Cadets and their lackeys, said that Germany would ignore us – but it has turned out otherwise and we already have the assent of Germany and Austria-Hungary to the holding of peace parleys and preliminary peace on the Soviet formula. And even before that, as soon as we obtained the keys to the case of secret diplomatic correspondence, we published the secret treaties thus fulfilling an obligation that we had assumed towards the people when we were still an insignificant opposition party. We said then and we say now that a people cannot shed their blood and that of their brothers for treaties that they have not themselves concluded, have never read or even seen. To these words of mine the adherents of the coalition replied: Do not speak to us in this tongue, this is not the Modern Circus. And I answered them that I have only one tongue, the tongue of a Socialist, and I shall speak in this tongue to the country and to you, to the Allies and to the Germans.

To the adherents of the coalition, having the souls of hares, it seemed that to publish the secret treaties was equivalent to forcing England and France to declare war on us. But they did not understand that their ruling circles throughout the duration of the war have been talking the people into the idea that the treacherous, cruel enemy is Germany and that Russia is a noble land, and it is impossible within twenty-four hours to teach them the opposite. By publishing the secret treaties we have incurred the enmity of the governing classes in those countries, but we have won their people to our support. We shall not make a diplomatic peace; it will be a people's peace, a soldiers' peace, a real peace. And the outcome of our open policy was clear: Judson appeared at the Smolny Institute and declared, in the name of America, that the protest to the Dukhonin staff against the new power was a misunderstanding and that America had no desire to interfere in the internal affairs of Russia; and, consequently, the American question is disposed of.

But there is another conflict that is not yet settled. I must tell you about it. Because of their fight for peace, the English government has arrested and is now detaining in a concentration camp George Chicherin, who has devoted his wealth and his knowledge to the peoples of Russia, England, Germany, and France, and the courageous agitator of the English workers, the emigré Petrov. I communicated in writing with the English embassy, saying that Russia was now permitting the presence within her borders of many wealthy Englishmen who are engaged in counter-revolutionary conspiracies with the Russian bourgeoisie, and that we were therefore all the more disinclined to permit Russian citizens to be thrown into English prisons; that, consequently, all those against whom there were no criminal charges should be liberated at once. Failure to comply with this request will mean that we shall refuse passports to English subjects desiring to leave Russia. The people's Soviet power is responsible for the well-being of the entire people; wherever its citizens may be, they shall enjoy its protection. If Kerensky spoke to the Allies like a shop attendant to his boss, we are prepared to show that we shall live with them only on terms of equality. We have more than once said that anyone who counts on the support and friendship of the free and independent Russian people must approach them with respect for them and for their human dignity.

As soon as the Soviets found themselves with power in their hands we proposed peace parleys in the name of the Russian people. We had a right to speak in the name of the people for everything that we proposed, as well as the whole programme of the People's Commissars, consists of doctrines and propositions voted on and passed in hundreds and thousands of Soviets, factories and workshops, that is, by the entire people. Our delegation will speak an open and courageous language: Do you agree to the holding of an immediate peace conference on all the fronts? And if they say yes, we shall ask them to invite their governments and allies to send their delegates. Our second question will be: Do you mean to conclude peace on a democratic foundation? If we are forced to make peace alone, we shall declare to

Germany that it is inadmissible to withdraw their troops from the Russian front to some other front, since we are offering an honourable peace and cannot permit England and France to be crushed by reason of it.

Secret diplomacy shall not be tolerated for a single moment during the negotiations. Our leaflets and our radio service will keep all the nations informed of every proposition we make and of the answers they elicit from Germany. We shall be sitting in a glass house, as it were, and the German soldiers, through thousands of newspapers in German, which we shall distribute to them, will be informed of every step we take and of every German answer.

We say that Lithuania and Courland must themselves decide with whom they will join forces, and that Germany must, not in words only but in deeds, heed the free expression of the will of the people. And if after these frank and honourable declarations the kaiser refuses to make peace, if the banks and exchanges, which profit by the war, destroy our peace, the nations will see on whose side is the right and we shall come out the stronger, the kaiser and the financiers the weaker. We shall feel ourselves to be not the vanquished but the victors, for peace has its victories no less renowned than war. For a nation that has assumed power after having cast out its enemies, such a nation is victorious. We know no other interests than those of the people, but these interests are identical with the interests of the people of all nations. We declare war upon war. The czars are afraid of the conclusion of peace, are afraid that the people will ask for an accounting for all the great sacrifices they have made and the blood they have shed. Germany, in agreeing to peace negotiations, is heeding the will of her people; she knows that they want her to answer, and that if she does not answer the Russian Revolution will become the ally of the German people. France and England ought to come to the discussion on the conclusion of peace, but if they do not their own people, who will know of the course of the transactions, will cast them out with rods. The Russian representatives at the peace table will be transformed into plaintiffs; the people will sit in judgement on their rulers. Our experience of the manner in which the rulers have treated their people in the forty months of the war has not been wasted. In your name we shall say to our brothers: Understand that the moment you turn your revolutionary strength against your bourgeoisie not one Russian soldier will shoot! This promise will be given in your name and you will keep it.

15. An Appeal to the Toiling, Oppressed and Exhausted Peoples of Europe

Pronouncement by Trotsky on December 6, 1918, during peace negotiations with the Central Powers at Brest-Litovsk.

An armistice has been signed at Brest-Litovsk. Military operations on the eastern front have been suspended for twenty-eight days. This in itself is a tremendous victory for humanity. After nearly three and a half years of uninterrupted slaughter, with no end in sight, the workers' and peasants' revolution in Russia has opened the way to peace.

We have published the secret treaties. We shall continue publishing them in the immediate future. We have declared that these treaties will in no way bind the policy of the Soviet government. We have proposed to all nations the way of open agreement on the principle of the recognition for each nation, great or small, advanced or backward, of the right freely to determine its own destiny. We do not attempt to conceal the fact that we do not consider the existing capitalist governments capable of making a democratic peace. The revolutionary struggle of the toiling masses against the existing governments can alone bring Europe nearer to such a peace. Its full realization can only be guaranteed by the victorious proletarian revolution in all capitalist countries.

While entering into negotiations with the existing governments, which on both sides are permeated through and through with imperialist tendencies, the Council of People's Commissars has never for a moment deviated from the path of social revolution. A truly democratic people's peace will still have to be fought for. The first round in this struggle finds in power, everywhere except in Russia, the old monarchist and capitalist governments which were responsible for the present war, and which have not yet accounted to their duped peoples for the waste of blood and riches. We are forced to begin negotiations with the governments which are now in existence, just as, on the other hand, the monarchist and reactionary governments of the Central Powers are forced to carry on negotiations with the representatives of the Soviet government because the Russian people have confronted them with the fact of a workers' and peasants' government in Russia. In negotiating for peace the Soviet government has set itself a double task: first, to bring to an end as quickly as possible the disgraceful and criminal slaughter which is laying Europe waste; and second, to use all the means at our disposal to help the working class in all lands to overthrow the rule of capital and to seize political power in order to reconstruct Europe and the whole world on democratic and socialist lines.

An armistice has been signed on the eastern front. But on the other fronts the slaughter is still going on. Peace negotiations are only just beginning. It should be clear to Socialists in all countries, but especially to socialists in Germany, that there is an irreconcilable difference between the peace programme of the Russian workers and peasants and that of the German capitalists, land-owners, and generals. If there were nothing but the clash of these two policies, peace would obviously be impossible, for the Russian people have not overthrown the monarchy and bourgeoisie in their own land merely to bow before the monarchs and capitalists of other lands. Peace can only be brought nearer, realized, and guaranteed if the voice of the workers makes itself heard, firmly and resolutely, both in Germany and in the lands of its allies. The German, Austro-Hungarian, Bulgarian, and Turkish workers must oppose to the imperialist programme of their ruling classes their own revolutionary programme of agreement and cooperation between the labouring and exploited classes in all countries.

An armistice has been signed on one front only. Our delegation, after a long struggle, wrung from the German government, as one of the conditions of the armistice, a commitment not to transfer troops to other fronts. Thus, those German troops which are stationed between the Black Sea and the Baltic are to have a month's respite from the gruesome nightmare of war. The Rumanian army also, against the will of the Rumanian government, adhered to the armistice. But on the French, Italian, and all other fronts the war is still going on. The truce remains partial. The capitalist governments fear peace, because they know they will have to render an account to their people. They are trying to postpone the hour of their final bankruptcy. Are the nations willing to go on patiently enduring the criminal activities of stock exchange cliques in France, Great Britain, Italy, and the United States?

The capitalist governments of these countries conceal their abject and greedy calculations under fine talk about eternal justice and the future society of nations. They do not want an armistice. They are fighting against peace, but you, peoples of Europe, you, workers of France, Italy, England, Belgium, Serbia, you, our brothers in suffering and struggle, do not you, together with us, want peace – an honourable, democratic peace among nations?

Those who tell you that peace can only be guaranteed by victory are deceiving you. In the first place they have been unable, in the course of nearly three and a half years, to give you victory, and show no signs of doing so should the war go on for years longer. And in the second place, if victory should appear possible for one side or the other, it would only mean further coercion of the weak by the strong, thus sowing the seeds of future wars.

Belgium, Serbia, Rumania, Poland, the Ukraine, Greece, Persia, and Armenia can only be liberated by the workers in all belligerent and neutral countries in the victorious struggle against all imperialists, and not by the victory of one of the imperialist coalitions.

We summon you to this struggle, workers of all countries! There is no other way. The crimes of the ruling, exploiting classes in this war have been countless. These crimes cry out for revolutionary revenge. Toiling humanity would be forswearing itself and its future if it continued meekly to bear on its shoulders the yoke of the imperialist bourgeoisie and militarists, their governments and their diplomacy.

We, the Council of People's Commissars, empowered by the Russian workers, peasants, soldiers, sailors, widows, and orphans, we summon you to a common struggle with us for the immediate cessation of hostilities on all fronts. May the news of the signing of the armistice at Brest-Litovsk ring like a tocsin for the soldiers and workers in all the belligerent countries.

Down with the war! Down with its authors! The governments opposing peace and the governments masking aggressive intentions behind talk of peace must be swept away. The workers and soldiers must wrest the business of war and peace from the criminal hands of the bourgeoisie and take it into their own hands. We have the right to demand this from you because this is what we have done in our own country. This is the only path to salvation for you and for us. Close up your ranks, proletarians of all countries, under the banner of peace and the social revolution!

16. *A Word to the Russian Workers and Peasants on Our Friends and Enemies, How to Preserve and Strengthen the Soviet Republic*

Faced with civil war and invasion by the Allies, the Bolsheviks appointed Trotsky commissar of war in March 1918. He gave this speech in Moscow on April 14, in the wake of having the previous month signed the punitive Brest-Litovsk treaty with the Central Powers that ended Russia's formal involvement in the First World War and in the wake of arrests of anarchists across Moscow.

Comrades – Our country is the only one where power is in the hands of the working class and on all sides we hear the advice: 'Leave it alone, you are not equal to the task. Look how many difficulties there are in the way of Soviet power.' And that is true, many are the difficulties, every step is beset with impediments. But what is the cause? Let us look around, let us examine the situation, let us count our friends and our enemies, let us look ahead. We inherited from our predecessors, the czar, Miliukov, Kerensky – *a state completely ruined internally as well as externally.* There is not the slightest doubt that at the present moment our country is in a terrible condition. But this condition is only the result of the whole of the preceding historical development and, in particular, of the present war. The czar and Miliukov had dragged us into the war. The czar's army was defeated. The revolution broke out. The toilers of all lands expected that the revolution would give peace. But Miliukov and Kerensky allowed themselves to be led on the leash by the Allied imperialists; they protracted the war, they deceived all expectations, and they compromised the revolution. Then the workers rebelled and took the power into their own hands. We on our part did everything that was possible to raise confidence in the Russian Revolution, to make it clear to the European workers that it was not Miliukov or Kerensky who represented the Russian Revolution, but the working class, the toiling proletariat, the peasant who did not exploit other people's labour.

This is what we did. It is true, comrades, the victory is not yet ours. We deceive neither ourselves nor you. European militarism has proved still too strong, the movement of the working masses has not yet dealt it that blow which will bring salvation to the European workers as well as to us, and European militarism has made the best use of the delay which history has granted it. The Russian Revolution has reached its summit, whereas the European one has not yet begun. It is in these conditions that our negotiations with Germany and Austria-Hungary took place, after the confidence in the Russian Revolution had been undermined by the policy of the Miliukovs, the Kerenskys, the Tseretellis, and the Chernovs. We are told: 'You have signed the Brest-Litovsk treaty, which is a predatory and oppressive treaty.' True, very true, there is no treaty so predatory, so oppressive as the Brest-Litovsk treaty. But what really is this treaty? It is an IOU, an old IOU which had already been signed by Nicholas Romanov, Miliukov, and Kerensky, while we have to pay it.

Was it we who started this war? Was it the working class who unchained this bloody slaughter? No, it was the monarchs, the wealthy classes, the liberal bourgeoisie. Was it we who caused those terrible disasters when our unfortunate soldiers found themselves in the Carpathians without rifles and ammunition? No, that was czarism supported by the Russian bourgeoisie.

And was it we who, on July 1, 1917, threw away in that shameful and criminal offensive the capital of the Russian Revolution, its good name, its authority? No, those were the Compromisers, the Right Social Revolutionaries, the Mensheviks, together with the bourgeoisie. Yet it is we who were presented with the bill for all these crimes, and we with clenched teeth were obliged to pay it. We know that it was a usurer's bill, but, comrades, it was not we who contracted the loans, it is not we who are morally responsible for them before the people. Our conscience is perfectly clear. We stand before the working class of all countries as a party which did its duty to the end. We published all the treaties, we sincerely declared that we were willing to conclude an honest democratic peace. This declaration remains, this idea remains in the consciousness and conscience of the toiling masses of Europe, and there it is accomplishing its deep subterranean work.

It is true, comrades, that at the present moment the frontiers of our country are secure neither in the East nor in the West. Over there in the East, Japan has for a long time past been trying to grab from us the most fertile, the richest parts of Siberia, and the Japanese press is only concerned as to the territorial limit up to which Japan is called upon to 'save' Siberia. The papers actually say so: 'We shall have to answer before God and Heaven for the fate of Siberia.' Some say that heaven enjoined them to grab Siberia up to Irkutsk, others say, up to the Urals. This is the only point of dispute among the propertied classes of Japan. They had been looking out for all sorts of pretexts to make this raid. As a matter of fact this business began long ago. Already under czarism, and later at the time of Tereshchenko and Kerensky, Russia was complaining in confidential documents that Japan was preparing for the seizure of our Far Eastern dominions. And why? Simply because they are an easy prey. This is indeed the whole essence of international imperialism. All those fine phrases about 'democracy', 'the fate of small nationalities', 'justice', 'God's commands' – all these are but words, phrases used for the purpose of cheating the common people; in reality the powers are only looking out for unprotected booty in order to pocket it. This I say is the essence of imperialist policy.

And so, comrades, at first, about six weeks ago, the Japanese spread throughout the world the rumour that the Siberian railway was about to be seized by the German and Austro-Hungarian prisoners who, forsooth, had been organized and armed there, and that 200,000 of them were only awaiting the arrival of a German general. Even the name of that general was given –

everything was perfectly definite and exact. The Japanese ambassador in Rome spoke about it, and the tidings of the coming seizure of the Siberian railway was circulated by the wireless stations of the Japanese headquarters throughout the length and breadth of America. Thereupon, in order to unveil before the public gaze of the entire world the shameful lie which has been spread for the purpose of preparing a buccaneering raid, I made the following offer to the British and American military missions: 'Give me one British and one American officer and I shall send them immediately, together with representatives of our commissariat of war, along the Siberian railway in order that they may see for themselves how many there are of German and Austrian prisoners armed for the purpose of seizing the Siberian railroads.'

They were unable, comrades, in all decency to refuse this offer, and the officers appointed by them went, having received from me papers ordering the Siberian Soviets to afford them all possible facilities: let them examine everything, see everything they wanted to see, get complete and free access everywhere. I afterwards was shown their reports every day by direct wire. It goes without saying that nowhere could they find even a trace of armed enemy prisoners. They saw that, different from the Russian railway system, the Siberian line was guarded better, and was working better. They only found 600 armed Hungarian prisoners who were Socialist internationalists, and had put themselves at the entire disposal of the Soviet authorities against all its enemies. That was all they found there. It proved up to the hilt that the

Japanese imperialists and the Japanese headquarters had consciously and maliciously misled public opinion in order to justify the predatory raid upon Siberia, in order to be able to say: the Germans had threatened the Siberian line, and we, the Japanese, rescued it by our raid. Well, *this* subterfuge failed; so immediately another was concocted on the spot. At Vladivostok somebody had killed two or three Japanese. No inquiry into the affair had as yet taken place. Who were the murderers? Were they Japanese agents, or common bandits, or German or Austrian spies? Nobody knows to this day. Yet though they were killed on April 4, the Japanese disembarked the first two companies at Vladivostok on April 5. Once the fairy tale about the seizure of the Siberian railway by the German prisoners proved of no avail, the simplest thing was to take advantage of the murder of two or three Japanese – killed, in all probability, on instructions from the Japanese headquarters itself in order to create a plausible pretext for attacking us. Such murders from behind a corner are the accepted practice of international capitalist diplomacy. But here the thing came to a sudden stop; two companies were disembarked and then the landing was discontinued. British, French, and American agents came to our commissariats and declared: 'This is not banditry or even a beginning of banditry and annexation, it is just a local incident, a local temporary misunderstanding'; as a matter of fact, it does seem as if the Japanese themselves were hesitating. First, their own country is exhausted by militarism, and an expedition against Siberia is a great, complicated, and costly affair, for the Siberian worker and peasant, the strong and sturdy peasant whom I studied closely enough in previous times and who never knew serfdom, would clearly refuse to let the Japanese take him without an effort. A long and stubborn fight would be necessary there; there is, indeed, in Japan itself a party which fears it. On the other hand, the American capitalists who directly compete with Japan on the shores of the Pacific do not want the strengthening of Japan, their chief enemy.

This, then, comrades, is the advantage of our position: the world bandits and highwaymen are at loggerheads with one another, fighting among themselves for the booty. This rivalry between Japan and the United States on the Far Eastern shores constitutes a great boon to us, for it gives us a respite, gives us an opportunity to gather our forces and to await the moment when the European and world working class will rise to help us.

In the West, comrades, we observe just now a new flaring up of the terrible slaughter which has already lasted five and forty months. It seemed before as if the forces of hell had already been set in motion, that nothing more could be invented, that the war had landed in a blind alley. If the countries, who had fought before with their forces still unimpaired, could not overpower one another, it seemed that there was nothing more to wait for, that no victory could be hoped for anywhere. But that is just the curse, that the wizard of capitalism, having called out this war devil, is powerless to exorcise him again. It is impossible, say, for the German bourgeoisie to come back to their workers and tell them: Well, we have conducted this terrible war for four years;

you have borne many sacrifices, and what has this war brought you? Nothing, absolutely nothing! Nor can the British bourgeoisie go back to its workers having a like result to show for all their unheard-of sacrifices.

That is why they are dragging on this slaughter automatically, senselessly, aimlessly, further and further. Just as an avalanche rolls down a mountain, so do they roll down under the weight of their own crimes.

This we observe now once more on the soil of unhappy white-bled France. There, comrades, on the French soil, the front is of a different nature than it was in our country. There every yard is studied beforehand, registered, placed on the map, every square distinctly marked. There colossal means of destruction, colossal monstrous engines for mass murders are collected on both sides on a scale hitherto inconceivable to the most powerful imagination.

Comrades, I lived in France for two years during the war, and I well remember those flowings and ebbings of attacks, and then the slow periods of waiting. An army stands against an army clasped tightly with one another, a trench against a trench, everything calculated, made ready. French public opinion becomes restive. Foch, the bourgeoisie, and the people in general begin grumbling. 'How much longer will this terrible constrictor, the front, be sucking the lifeblood of the people? Where is the way out? What are we waiting for? Either stop the war or else vanquish the enemy by an offensive and get peace. Either one or the other.' The bourgeois press would then begin its encouragements: 'The next offensive, tomorrow, the day after tomorrow, next spring, will deal the Germans a mortal blow.'

At the same time no less corrupt and mercenary pens would be writing in the German press for the benefit of the German workers and peasants, for the German mothers, workingwomen, sisters, wives: 'Do not despair, one other offensive on the French front and we shall crush France and will give you peace.' Thereupon, in fact, an offensive would begin.

Countless victims, hundreds, thousands, millions would perish in the course of a few days or weeks. And the result? As a result, the front would be shifted one way or another a mile or two, perhaps even more, but the two armies would continue as before to press against one another in a death clasp; and so it has happened already five or six times. It was so on the Marne during the first rush upon Paris, the same later, on the Yser, then on the Somme, at Cambrai. The same thing is now taking place in the present colossal battles, such as were never before witnessed throughout the whole of history. Hundreds of thousands, millions are falling there at the present moment, the flower of European humanity is being destroyed senselessly, aimlessly. This shows that there is no salvation on the road on which the ruling classes and their lackeys, the pseudosocialists, walk.

America joined the war more than a year ago, and promised to finish it in the course of the next few months. What did America get by her intervention? She had at first been patiently waiting over there, beyond the ocean, while Germany was fighting England; and then she intervened. Why? What does America want? America wants Germany to exhaust England, and England to exhaust Germany. Then American capital will come forward as an heir who will rob the whole world. And so when America noticed that England was being bent to the ground, and that Germany was getting the upper hand, she said: 'So, it is necessary to support England – just as the rope supports the one hanged – in order that they may exhaust each other completely, in order that European capital may be deprived of all possibility to stand up again on its feet.' And at the present moment we read that in Washington, according to the new conscription law, one and a half million men are to be called to arms.

America at first thought the business would be a trifling one, would just amount to a little help; but as soon as she placed her feet on the path, the avalanche caught her in its sweep, and now there is no stopping for her either, and she must go to the bitter end. And yet – at the beginning of the war, at the beginning of the American intervention – that happened in January or February of last year – I myself saw a street demonstration in New York, a downright revolt of the American workingmen, caused by a terrible rise of prices. The American bourgeoisie has earned billions from the blood of the European worker; but what did the American housewife, the workingwoman, get? Her share is scarcity, and the tremendous cost of living. It is the same in all countries, whether the bourgeoisie of one or the other country wins or suffers defeat. For the workers, the toiling masses, the result is the same: exhaustion of food stocks, impoverishment, enhanced slavery and oppression, accidents, wounds, cripples – all this pours upon the popular masses. The bourgeoisie itself can no longer choose its way – that is precisely why Germany did not strangle us completely. She stopped at the Eastern front. Why? Because she had yet to settle her accounts with England and America. England has taken Egypt, Palestine, Baghdad, has brought under her sway Portugal, has strangled Ireland, but – England 'fights for freedom, for peace, for the happiness of small and weak nationalities'. And Germany? Germany has robbed half of Europe, has suppressed scores of small countries, has taken Riga, Reval, and Pskov. Yet read their speeches: they declare that they have concluded peace on the basis of self-determination of peoples! First they bleed the people white, turn it into a corpse, and then they say: Now it has determined itself that Germany should lay her hand upon it.

Such is the position of the Russian Revolution, of the Russian Soviet Republic. Dangers threaten her on all sides: in the East there is the Japanese peril, in the West the German peril, and of course, there is for us also, although not so close, the British and American perils. All these strong, powerful bandits would not at all mind tearing Russia to pieces, and if at the present moment, today, we have some guarantee against it, it consists in the fact that these countries could not come to an understanding with one another, that Japan is compelled to carry on a veiled, underground struggle against such a mighty power as the United States, while Germany is compelled to conduct an open bloody struggle against both England and the United States.

And so, comrades, at a time when the world bandits have come to grips in the last convulsive round, honest people get a chance of having a rest, of recuperating, of refreshing themselves, of arming, in expectation of the hour when the working class will inflict upon these world bandits the mortal blow.

From the very first days of the revolution we said that the Russian Revolution would be able to win and to free the Russian people only on the condition that it marked the beginning of a revolution in all countries, but that if in Germany the reign of capital remained, if in New York the supremacy of the stock exchange continued, if in England British imperialism held its sway as heretofore, then we should be done for, since they were stronger, richer than we, as yet better educated, and their military machines stronger than ours. They would strangle us, because – number one – they were the stronger, and because – number two – they hated us. We had revolted, we had overthrown in our country the rule of the bourgeoisie. That is the source of the hatred towards us on the part of the propertied classes of all countries. Our bourgeoisie cannot be compared to the bourgeoisie of Germany or England. Yonder it is a strong class, it has a past of its own, when it made cultural conquests, developed science, and thought that no one but itself could hold sway, no one but itself could rule the state.

Every genuine bourgeois thinks that nature itself has

destined him to dominate, to command, ride on the backs of the toiling masses, while the worker lives day in, day out under a yoke, and his horizon is narrow. With his mother's milk he has imbibed slavish prejudices, and thinks that to govern the state, to hold power is quite beyond him, that he was not meant for it, that he is made of poorer stuff.

But, lo and behold, the workers and poorer peasants in Russia have made the first step – a good firm step, though only the first one – in order to put an end to the propertied classes of their own as well as of all other countries. They have shown that the working masses are made of the same stuff of which people in general are made, and that they want to hold in their own hands the whole power and govern the whole land. Naturally when the bourgeoisie saw that in taking this power we were in dead earnest, that we meant business, namely, to destroy the domination of capital and to put in its place the domination of labour, its hatred towards us began to swell prodigiously. At first the propertied classes, the exploiters, thought that this was only a temporary misunderstanding, that it was only a stray wave of the revolution which had given us a mighty swing, and only, as it were, by accident had lifted us up, that the workers had got hold of the power only for a time, and that all that would end in a week, or two, or three. But later on it dawned upon them that the workers were standing firm at their new posts and while saying that times were hard, that still greater trials were in prospect, still greater ruin, still more intense hunger would have to be suffered, yet once they had assumed power, they would never let it escape from their hands. Never!

The bourgeoisie in all countries then began to notice that a terrible infection was spreading from the east, from Russia. Indeed, after the Russian worker, the most ignorant, most overdriven and harassed of all, has taken the power into his own hands, those of other countries must necessarily say to themselves sooner or later: if the Russian workers, who are so much the poorer, weaker, less organized than ourselves, could take the power into their own hands, then if we, the advanced workers of the whole world, seize the Russian cudgel and shake off our own bourgeoisie, and organize the whole of industry, verily, we shall then be invincible and shall create a universal republic of labour.

Yes, comrades, we are feared; we stand before the conscience of the propertied classes as a spectre. The British imperialists fight the Germans, but every now and then they anxiously look round at us with the intent of getting at the throat of the Russian Revolution. In a similar way German imperialism, chained as it is to its enemy, cannot help sending us from time to time a furtive glance, trying to find a favourable opportunity to stab us in the heart. The imperialists of all other countries are of similar mind. No national difference exists on this point, since the common interests of the bandits and beasts of prey unite them all against us, and let me remind you, comrades, that we always told you that if the revolution did not spread to other countries, we shall in the long run be crushed by European capitalism. No escape will be available, and our task at the present moment is to procrastinate, to hold out till the revolution begins in all European countries – to hold out, to consolidate our strength, and to stand firmer on our feet, since at present we are feeble, shattered and morally feeble.

We ourselves know our sins, and we do not need the criticism from outside, from the bourgeoisie and the Compromisers who have undermined the Russian state and economic life; their criticism is not worth two pence. But we do need our own criticism in order that we may realize our own sins. And in this connection the following must be said above everything else: the Russian working class, the Russian toiling people, must realize that once it took over the power in the state, it assumed the responsibility for the fate of the whole country, of the whole economic life of the whole state.

Of course, even now the bourgeoisie and its lackeys are still trying to put spokes in our wheels. Therefore, each time they stand in our way, we shall as heretofore fling them aside. At Orenburg they are again sending their Dutovs against us; Kornilov, too, tries to attack Rostov. There we shall deal with the gangs of bourgeois White Guards without mercy. This is a matter of course for all of us. In this respect there will be no change in our tactics. If the bourgeoisie still hopes to come back into power we shall once for all knock out of it that hope. If it rises, we shall fling it down again, and if, as a result, it breaks its neck – so much the worse for it. It is its own lookout. It has had its warnings.

We offer it the common fare, the universal labour duty – a labour regime without oppressed or oppressors, and if it does not like it, if it continues to be obdurate and to revolt, the Soviet power must use against it measures of repression.

But, comrades, just because we, all of us as one man, do not want to allow the restoration of the power of the bourgeoisie, of the squires, of the bureaucracy, and because we are prepared to stand up for the power of the working class and the poorest peasants to the last drop of our blood, we must say to ourselves that from today we shoulder the greatest task and must therefore establish in our country a settled order, a new labour regime. We have inherited from the past, from czardom, from the war, from the Miliukov–Kerensky period a complete dislocation of our railways, a dislocation of our factories, and of all the branches of economic and social life, and we must put all this in working order, for we are responsible for it all.

The Soviets, the trade unions, the peasant organizations – these are at the present moment the masters in the country. Formerly, comrades, we were living under a whip, the whip of bureaucracy; but that whip is no more. There are only organizations of workers and the poorest peasants, and these organizations must teach us all to know and to remember that every one of us is not an isolated unit, but before all a part of the working class, of a common great association the name of which is 'Toiling Russia' and which can only be saved by common labour. When the railwaymen surreptitiously carry a load; when depots or, in general, state property is plundered by individuals, we must denounce it as the greatest crime against our people – against the revolution. We must keep a sleepless watch and tell such betrayers, 'You rob the propertyless classes – not the bourgeoisie, but yourself, your own people!' At the present moment every one of us, whatever post he occupies in a factory or on the railways – everywhere he ought to feel himself like a soldier who has been placed there by the workers' army, by his own people, and every one of us must discharge his duty to the end.

This new labour discipline, comrades, we must create at all costs. Anarchy will destroy us; labour order will save us. In the factories we must create elected tribunals to punish the shirkers. Every worker, once he has become the master of his country, must distinctly remember his labour duty and his labour honour. Every one of us must fulfil one and the same obligation: 'I work a certain number of hours a day with all the energy, with all the application I am capable of for now my labour is for the common good. I work in order to equip the peasant with the necessary implements of labour. I create for him winnowing machines, ploughs, scythes, nails, horseshoes, everything that is necessary for agriculture, and the peasant must give me bread.'

Here, comrades, we are approaching the question of grain – the most acute question with us at the present moment. There is a lack of grain. The towns are starving, yet the present bourgeoisie, the usurers somewhere in the Tula, Orel, Kursk, or other provinces have concentrated in their hands enormous quantities of grain, tens of millions of poods, and resolutely refuse to surrender it, keep it in their grasp and resist all attempts at requisition.

They let the grain rot, while in the towns and grainless provinces the workers and peasants starve. At the present moment the village bourgeoisie is becoming the chief enemy of the working class. It wants to defeat the Soviet resolutions by means of starvation, in order to usurp the land. They, the village usurers, the bloodsuckers, understand that the Socialist revolution spells death for them. There are many, these village usurers, in various parts of the country, and our task at present is to show the poorest peasants everywhere that their interests are deadly opposed to the interests of the rich peasants, and that if the village usurers win, they will grab all the land, and new squires will appear – this time not members of the nobility, but of the class of village usurers. It is necessary that in the villages the poorest peasants should unite with the town workers against the village and town bourgeoisie, against the village usurers and bloodsuckers. These usurers hold up the grain, hoard up the money, and try to grab all the land; and if they succeed, the poorest peasants and the entire revolution are done for. We warn the village usurers that we shall be ruthless towards them. It is here a question of the feeding of the towns, of not allowing our children in the towns, our old mothers, our old men, our workingmen and women in the towns, and our breadless provinces to go without their daily bread. Once it is a question of life or death for the toilers, we shall allow no jokes. We shall not be stopped by the interests of the village bourgeoisie, but, together with the town and village poor, we shall lay a heavy hand upon the property of the village bourgeoisie and shall forcibly requisition without compensation its grain stores in order to feed the poor in the towns and villages.

But in order to carry out a firm policy with respect to our enemies, we must introduce a firm order into our own midst. The thing is, comrades, that a lot of frivolity, inexperience, and dishonesty has appeared in the midst of the uneducated sections of the working class. We must not shut our eyes to it. Some workers argue: 'Why should I try my hardest now? Everything is broken up, and whether I do or don't work hard, things won't change on account of that.' Such an attitude is criminal. We must strengthen within us the sense of responsibility, so that every one of us should say: 'If I do not fulfil my duty, the whole machine will work still worse.' All must create a sense of labour discipline, of labour duty, and joint responsibility. I am instructed, comrades, by the Central Executive Committee to undertake the task of creating a properly equipped army for the defence of Socialist Russia. But the Red Army will be powerless, thrice powerless, if our railways are bad, if our mills and factories are ruined, and if food is not brought in from the villages to the towns.

It is necessary to get to work to strengthen Soviet Russia on all sides, conscientiously and honestly. A firm order must be established everywhere. Our Red Army must be permeated by the new aim of being the armed advance guard of the labouring people. The mission of the Red Army is to defend the state authority of the workers and peasants. This is the highest possible mission. And for such a mission discipline is necessary, a firm, an iron discipline. Formerly there existed a discipline for the defence of the czar, the landowners, the capitalists, but now every Red soldier must say to himself that the new discipline is one in the service of the working class; and we together with you, comrades, shall introduce a new Soviet Socialist oath, not in the name of God or czar, but in the name of the labouring people, that in case of violation of, or raid, or attack upon the rights of the labouring people, upon the power of the proletariat and the poor peasants, he will be prepared to fight to the last drop of his blood. And you, all of you, the whole working class, will be witnesses of this oath, witnesses and participators of this solemn vow.

The first of May is approaching, comrades, and on that day we shall again gather together with the Red Army in great meetings, and shall take stock of what has been done, and ascertain what there is still to be done. And there is still a lot to be done.

Comrades, in preparation for the first of May, the Soviet government has decreed, where possible, the removal from the streets of the old czarist monuments, the old stone and metal idols which remind us of our slavery of the past. We shall then endeavour, comrades, to erect in the near future on our squares new monuments, monuments to labour, monuments to workers and peasants, monuments which will remind every one of you: look, you were a slave, you were nothing and now you must become everything, you must rise high, you must learn, you must become the master of all life.

Comrades, the misfortune of women is not only that they are ill-fed, ill-clothed – this is of course the greatest misfortune – but also that they are not allowed to rise mentally, to study, to develop. There are many spiritual values, lofty and beautiful. There are the sciences and the arts – and all this is inaccessible to the toilers, because workers and peasants are compelled to live like convicts, chained to their wheelbarrow. Their thought, their consciousness, their feelings, must be freed.

We must see to it that our children, our younger brothers have the opportunity of getting acquainted with all the conquests of the mind, with the arts and sciences, and be able to live as befits a human being who calls himself 'lord of creation', and not, as hitherto, like a wretched slave, crushed and oppressed. It is of all this that we shall be reminded by May Day when we must meet together with the Red Army and declare: We have taken the power into our hands and we shall not give it up, and this power is for us not an end in itself, but a means – a means for another grand object, which is to reconstruct the whole of life, to make all wealth, all the possibilities of happiness, accessible to the whole people; to establish at last, for the first time, such an order upon this earth as would do away, on the one hand, with the man bent and oppressed and, on the other, with him who rides on the back of his fellow men; to establish firmly a common cooperative economic system, a common labour party, so that all shall work for the common good, that the whole people shall live as one honest loving family.

All this we can and shall realize completely only when the European working class supports us.

Comrades, we should be wretched, blind men of little faith, if we even for one single day were to lose our conviction that the working class of other countries will come to our aid, and following our example, will rise and bring our task to a successful conclusion. You need only call to mind what the toiling masses are living through at the present moment – the soldier masses of Germany on the Western front, where a raging, hellish offensive is going on, where millions of our brothers are perishing on both sides of the front. Does not the same blood which runs in our veins run in the veins of the German workers? Do not the German widows weep in exactly the same way when their husbands perish, or the orphan children when their fathers are killed? The same poverty, the same starvation stalk there; the same un-happy cripples come back from the trenches into the towns and villages and wander like wretched worn-out shadows. Everywhere the war produces the same conse-quences. Dire want and poverty reign supreme in all lands. And the final result will be, in the long run, everywhere the same: the rising of the labouring masses.

The task of the German working class is more diffi-cult than ours, because the German state machine is stronger than ours, is made of stronger material than was the state of our czar of blessed memory. There the noblemen, the capitalists are robbers, just as ours, just as cruel; only there they are not drunkards, not idlers, not embezzlers of public funds, but efficient robbers, intelligent robbers, earnest robbers. There they have constructed a strong state boiler, which is pressed on all sides by the labouring masses, a boiler made of sound material, and the German working class will have to develop a good deal of steam before it explodes. The steam is already accumulating, as it was accumulating here, but since the boiler is stronger, more steam is needed. The day, however, will come, comrades, when that boiler will blow up, and then the working class will get hold of an iron broom and will start sweeping the dust out of all corners of the present German empire, and will do it with German thoroughness and steadiness, so that our hearts will rejoice watching them doing it.

But in the meantime we say: 'We are passing through hard, strenuous times, but we are prepared to suffer hunger, cold, rain, and many other calamities and misfortunes, because we are only part of the world working class and are fighting for its complete emancipation. And we shall hold out, comrades, and shall carry our fight to a successful end, we shall repair the railways, the locomotives, we shall put production on a firm basis, straighten out the food supply, do all that is necessary – if only we keep in our bodies a cheerful mind and a strong stout heart. So long as our soul is a living one, our Russian land is safe, and the Soviet Republic stands firm.'

Let us then, comrades, remember and remind the less conscious of us that we stand as a city on the mount, and that the workers of all countries look at us and ask themselves with bated breath, whether we shall tumble off or not, whether we fail or stand our ground. And we on our part call out to them: 'We vow to you that we shall stand our ground, that we shall not fail, that we shall remain in power to the end.' But you, workers of other countries, you, brothers, do not exhaust our patience too much, hurry up, stop the slaughter, over-throw the bourgeoisie, take the power into your hands, and then we shall turn the whole globe into one world republic of labour. All the earthly riches, all the lands, and all the seas – all this shall be one common property of the whole of humanity, whatever the name of its parts: English, Russian, French, German, etc. We shall create one brotherly state: the land which nature gave us. This land we shall plough and cultivate on cooperative principles, turn into one blossoming garden, where our children, grandchildren, and great-grandchildren will live as in a paradise. Time was when people believed in legends which told of a paradise. These were vague and confused dreams, the yearning of the soul of oppressed man after a better life. There was the yearning after a purer, more righteous life, and man said: 'There must be such a paradise, at least in the "other" world, an unknown and mysterious country.' But we say, we shall create such a paradise with our toiling hands *here*, in *this* world, upon *earth*, for all, for our children and grandchildren and for all eternity!

[The chairman: It is evident that there is no opposition. Comrade Trotsky will answer questions.]

Comrades, there are a great number of questions

here, but I shall answer only those which are of general interest.

'Is it true that you wanted to introduce a ten-hour labour day?'

No, comrades, that is not true. Although this is spread, broadcast by the Mensheviks and the Right SRs, it is nevertheless a lie. It has arisen in the following way. At one of the meetings I said, 'Of course, if we should all of us work now eight hours a day conscientiously, as one ought to, and if we should put into the harness also the bourgeoisie and those who destroyed us yesterday on the strict principle of labour service, we could raise the wealth of our country to a very high degree in a very short time.' It is necessary, said I, to raise between ourselves a feeling of responsibility for the fate of the whole country, and to work with all our might, without rest or haste, just as in a family, for instance, where there is no bickering over the work to be done. If it is a good, honest family, its members will not say: 'I have done today more than you.' If any member should have more strength, he will work harder. At the same time everyone works in such a manner that if needs be they work sometimes even sixteen hours a day, since they work not for a master, nor for a capitalist, but for themselves. That is how the statement arose, that I wanted to substitute a ten- or even a sixteen-hour day for an eight-hour day. It is sheer nonsense. We say: there is no necessity for it. It will be sufficient if we could establish, through the trade unions and the Soviets, such a firm discipline that everybody should work eight hours

– by no means more, and as soon as possible, even seven hours – and that the work should be done conscientiously, that is, that every particle of labour time should be really filled with work, that everyone should know and remember that he works for a common association, for a common fund – that is all we are striving for, comrades.

I am asked further: *'You call yourselves Socialist Communists, and yet you shoot and imprison your comrades, the anarchist Communists?'*

This is a question, comrades, which, indeed, requires elucidation – a serious question, no doubt. We, Marxist Communists, are deeply at variance with the anarchist doctrine. This doctrine is erroneous, but that would not in any way justify arrests, imprisonment, not to speak of shootings.

I will first explain in a few words wherein the mistake of the anarchist doctrine lies. The anarchist declares that the working class needs no state power; what it does need is to organize production. State power, he says, is a bourgeois service. State power is a bourgeois machine, and the working class must not take it into its hands. This is a thoroughly mistaken view. When you organize your economic life in a village, generally in small areas, no state power, indeed, is required. But when you organize your economic system for the whole of Russia, for a big country – and however much they robbed us, we are still a big country – there is need for a state apparatus, an apparatus which was hitherto in the hands of a hostile class that exploited and robbed the toilers. We say: in order to organize production in a new manner, it is necessary to wrest the state apparatus, the government machine from the hands of the enemy and grasp it in our own hands. Otherwise nothing will come of it. Where does exploitation, oppression, come from? It comes from private property in the means of production. And who stands up for it, who supports it? The state, so long as it is in the hands of the bourgeoisie. Who can abolish private property? The state, as soon as it falls into the hands of the working class.

The bourgeoisie says: don't touch the state – it is a sacred hereditary right of the 'educated' classes. And the anarchists say: don't touch it – it is a hellish invention, a devilish machine, keep away from it. The bourgeoisie says: don't touch – it is holy; the anarchists say: don't touch – it is sinful. Both say: don't touch. But we say: we shall not only touch it, but take it over into our hands and run it in our own interests, for the abolition of private property, for the emancipation of the working class.

But, comrades, however mistaken the doctrine of the anarchists, it is perfectly inadmissible to persecute them for it. Many anarchists are perfectly honest champions of the working class; only they don't know how the lock can be opened, how to open the door into the kingdom of freedom, and they crowd at the door, elbowing one another, but unable to guess how to turn the key. But this is their misfortune, not their fault – it is not a crime, and they must not be punished for it.

But, comrades, during the period of the revolution, under the flag of anarchism – as everybody knows, and the honest idealist anarchist better than anybody else – a host of all sorts of hooligans, jailbirds, thieves, and night bandits have crowded in. Only yesterday the man served his term of hard labour for rape, or of prison for stealing, or was deported for banditry, and today he declares: 'I am an anarchist – a member of the club,' the 'Black Crow', the 'Tempest', the 'Storm', the 'Lava', etc., etc., a lot of names, a great lot.

Comrades, I have talked about it to the idealist anarchists, and they themselves say: 'A lot of these jailbirds, hooligans, and criminals have smuggled themselves into our movement . . .'

You all know what occurs in Moscow. Whole streets are forced to pay tribute. Buildings are seized over the heads of the Soviets, of the labour organizations, and it happens also that when the Soviets occupy a building, these hooligans under the mask of anarchists break into the building, fix up machine guns, seize armoured cars and even artillery. Lots of plunder, heaps of gold have been discovered in their nests. They are simply raiders and burglars who compromise the anarchists. Anarchism is an idea although a mistaken one, but hooliganism is hooliganism; and we told the anarchists: You must draw a strict line between yourselves and the burglars, for there is no greater danger to the revolution than when it begins to decay at any point, the whole tissue of the revolution will then go to pieces. The Soviet regime must be of firm texture. We took power not in order to plunder like some highwaymen and burglars, but in order to introduce a common labour discipline and an honest labour life.

I hold that the Soviet authorities acted quite correctly when they said to the pseudoanarchists: 'Don't imagine that your reign has come, don't imagine that the Russian people or the Soviet state is now a carrion upon which the crows alight to peck it to pieces. If you want to live together with us on the principles of common labour, then submit with us to the common Soviet discipline of the labouring class, but if you put yourselves in our way, then don't blame us if the labour government, the Soviet power, handles you without mittens.'

If the pseudoanarchists or, to be plain, the hooligans will attempt in the future to act in the same way, the second chastisement will be thrice, ten times as severe as the first. It is stated that among these hooligans there are a few who are honest anarchists; if that is true – and this looks as if it were true with respect to a few men – then it is a great pity, and it is necessary to render them their freedom as quickly as possible. It is necessary to express to them our sincere regret, but at the same time to tell them – Comrades, anarchists, in order that no such mistakes should occur in the future you must put between you and those hooligans a sort of watershed, a hard line in order that you should not be mixed up one with another, that one should know once for all: that is a burglar, and this is an honest idealist. . . .

[At this point a commotion, a noise, and a general confusion interrupt the speaker.]

[The chairman: Nothing extraordinary has happened. Some fifteen anarchists demonstratively left the hall.]

Order, comrades.

Well, comrades, we have just now seen, in a small way, an example of how a small group of men can break up solidarity and order. We were calmly discussing our common problems here. The platform was open to all. The anarchists had the right to demand their turn and speak, if they wanted. I spoke of the true anarchists without animosity or bitterness, as everybody can testify; more than that, I said that among the anarchists there are many mistaken friends of the working class, that they must not be arrested or shot. Against whom did I speak with rancour? Against the hooligans, who put on the mask of anarchism in order to destroy the order and life and labour of the working class. I don't know to what camp these persons belong who thought it possible to create at a crowded meeting a provocative scene of this sort, which frightened many of you and brought in confusion and chaos at our popular meeting.

I am also asked, comrades, '*Why is the elective principle being abolished in military service?*' I shall say a few words about it presently. It was necessary in our old army, which we inherited from czardom, to dismiss the old chiefs, generals and colonels, for in the majority of cases they had been the tools in the hands of a class hostile to us, in the hands of czardom and of the bourgeoisie. Hence when the soldier-workers and soldier-peasants need to elect commanders for themselves, they elected not military chiefs, but simply such representatives who could guard them against attacks of counter-revolutionary classes. But at the present time, comrades, who is building up the army? The bourgeoisie? No, the workers' and peasants' Soviets, i.e., the same classes which compose the army. Here no internal struggle is possible. Let us take as an instance the trade unions. The metal workers elect their committee, and the committee finds a secretary, a clerk, and a number of other persons who are necessary. Does it ever happen that the workers should say: 'Why are our clerks and treasurers appointed, and not elected?' No, no intelligent workers will say so. Otherwise the committee would say: 'You yourselves have chosen the committee. If you don't like us, dismiss us, but once you have entrusted us with the direction of the union, then give us the possibility of choosing the clerk or the cashier, since we are better able to judge in the matter than you, and if our way of conducting the business is bad, then throw us out and elect another committee.' The Soviet government is the same as the committee of a trade union. It is elected by the workers and peasants, and you can at the All-Russian Congress of the Soviets, at any moment you like, dismiss that government and appoint another. But once you have appointed it, you must give it the right to choose the technical specialists, the clerks, the secretaries in the broad sense of the word and, in military affairs, in particular. For is it possible for the Soviet government to appoint military specialists against the interests of the labouring and peasant masses? Besides, there is no other way at the present, no other way open, but the way of appointment. The army is now only in the process of formation. How could soldiers who have just entered the army choose the chiefs! Have they any vote to go by? They have none. And therefore elections are impossible.

Who appoints the commanders? The Soviet government appoints them. Registers are kept of former officers and prominent individuals from among the ranks and non-commissioned officers who have shown capacity. Candidates receive their appointments out of this register. If they do represent some danger, there are the commissars to look after them. What is a commissar? The commissars are appointed from among Bolsheviks or the Left SRs, that is from the parties of the working class and of the peasantry. These commissars do not intervene in military affairs. These are managed by military specialists, but commissars keep a sharp eye on them that they may not abuse their position against the interests of the workers or the peasants. And the commissars are invested with large powers of control and prevention of counter-revolutionary acts. If the military leader issues an order directed against the interests of the workers and peasants, the commissar will say, Stop! and will lay his hand on the order and the military leader. If the commissar will act unjustly, he will answer for it in strict accordance with law.

In the first period, comrades, up to October and during October we fought for the power of the labouring masses. Who stood in our way? It was, among others, the generals, the admirals, the sabotaging bureaucrats. What did we do? We fought them. Why? Because the working class was marching to power, and nobody ought to have dared prevent it from taking it. Now the power is in the hands of the working class. And so we say:

'Kindly step forward, gentlemen saboteurs, and place yourselves in the service of the working class.' We want to make them work, for they also represent a certain capital. They have learned something which we have not. The civil engineer, the medical man, the general, the admiral – they have all studied things which we have not studied. Without the admiral we could not manage a ship; we could not cure a sick person without the physician; and without the engineer we could not build a factory. And we say to all these persons: 'We need your knowledge and we shall summon you to the service of the working class.' And they will know that if they work honestly to the best of their abilities they will have the fullest scope for their work, and nobody will interfere with them. Quite the contrary: the working class is a sufficiently mature class and will give them every assistance in their work. But if they attempt to use their posts in the interests of the bourgeoisie and against us, we shall remind them of the October and other days.

The social order which we are now establishing is a labour social order, a regime of the working class and of the poorest peasants. We need every specialist and every intellectual if he is not a slave of the czar or of the bourgeoisie, and, if he is really a capable worker, he can come to us and we shall receive him openly and honestly. We shall work with him hand in hand, because he will serve the labouring master of his country. But as for those who sabotage, intrigue, idle, and lead a parasitical life – comrades, give us but the chance of putting our organization in good order, and we shall immediately pass and carry into effect a law for them: he who does not work, who resists, who sabotages – neither shall he eat. We shall take away the bread cards from all saboteurs, from all who undermine the labour discipline of the Soviet Republic.

I am also asked: *'Why are we not introducing free trade in grain?'* If at the present moment, comrades, we introduced free trade in grain, we should in a fortnight stand before the dreadful spectre of starvation. What would happen? There are provinces where there is plenty of grain, but where the peasant bourgeoisie does not sell it at the present time at fixed prices. If prices were freed from control, all the speculators, all the dealers would rush into those grain-producing provinces, and the grain prices would rise in the course of a few days or a few hours, and reach 50, 100, or 150 rubles a pood. Then these speculators would start snatching the grain from one another, flinging it on the railways, and snatching the trucks from one another. At present there is among our railway workers, especially of the higher grade, a lot of corruption; they sell wagons for money and take bribes. If free trade in grain were to be proclaimed, the speculators would pay still higher prices for the wagons, and we should get a still greater disorganization on the railways. And the grain which would arrive into the towns would be quite out of your reach, workers.

Of course, fixed prices for grain will not bring us salvation if firm discipline on the railways is not established. It is necessary to establish a stricter regime for the higher-grade workers and those who encourage bribery, embezzlement, and rapacity among them. And it is also necessary that the whole railway staff should redouble its energy.

Then we must show the village usurers that we are not in a mood for jesting; that it is their duty to surrender their stocks of grain at fixed prices. If they do not surrender them, these must be taken away from them by force – by the armed force of the poor peasants and workers. It is the life and death of the people which is in question and not the speculators and usurers.

The situation is distressing in the highest degree – and not only with us. Holland, for instance, is a neutral country. It did not take part in the war. Yet the other day telegrams arrived stating that in Amsterdam the ration has been reduced for the whole population, and a hunger riot took place in the streets. Why? Because instead of ploughing, sowing, and cutting, scores of millions of men throughout the world have been destroying one another all these last four years. All countries have been impoverished and exhausted, and so it is with us. Therefore, a certain time – a year or two – must pass before we renew our grain stocks, and in the meantime only labour, discipline, order and severe pressure upon the village usurers, the speculators, and the freebooters will help us. If we establish all this, then we shall hold out.

And now let me reply to the last question, comrades: *'Who is going to pay the indemnity to Germany in accordance with the Brest treaty?'*

How shall I say it, comrades? If the Brest-Litovsk treaty holds, then of course, the Russian people will pay.

If in other countries the same governments remain which are in existence now, then our revolutionary Russia will be well coffined and buried, and the Brest treaty will be followed by a new one, a Petrograd or Irkutsk treaty which will be thrice or ten times worse than the Brest treaty. The Russian Revolution and European imperialism cannot live side by side for a long time. For the present we exist because the German bourgeoisie carries on a bloody litigation with the English and French bourgeoisie. Japan is in rivalry with America and, therefore, in the meantime its hands are tied. That is why we keep above water. As soon as the plunderers conclude peace, they will all turn against us. And then Germany, together with England, will split the body of Russia in two. There can be no shadow of doubt about it. And the Brest-Litovsk treaty will have to go. A much more grievous, severe, more merciless treaty will be forced upon us. That is the case if European and American capitalists remain where they are, that is, if the working class will not budge from its present place. Then we are done for. And then, of course, the labouring Russian people will pay for everything, will pay with its blood, its labour, will pay during scores of years, from generation to generation. But, comrades, we have no right whatever to assume that after this war everything will remain in Europe as it was.

The working class in every country was deceived by their pseudosocialists, their own Right SRs, Mensheviks, the Scheidemanns, the Davids, and equivalents of our own Tseretellis, Kerenskys, Chernovs, Martovs. They have declared to the workers: 'You are not ripe yet for taking the power into your own hands, you must support the democratic bourgeoisie.' And the democratic bourgeoisie supports the big bourgeoisie, which supports the noblemen who in their turn support the kaiser. This is how the European Mensheviks and Right SRs found themselves chained to the chair of the kaiser, or to that of Poincaré during the war. And so, four years have passed. It is impossible to admit for one moment that after such a terrible experience of bloodletting, calamities, deceit, and exhaustion of the country, the working class, on leaving the trenches, all again humbly return to the factories and all slavishly, as in the days gone by, turn the wheel of capitalist exploitation. No. On coming out of the trenches it will present a bill to its masters. It will say: 'You have exacted from us a tribute of blood, and what have you given us instead? The old oppressors, the landowners, the oppression of capitalism, the bureaucracy!'

I repeat: If in the West capitalism remains, a peace will be forced upon us which will be ten times worse than the Brest-Litovsk peace. We shall not be able to stand on our legs. It is said that he who hopes for a European revolution is a utopian, a visionary, a dreamer. And I say: 'He who does not hope for a revolution in all countries prepares a coffin for the Russian people.' He virtually says: 'The party which possesses the most effective killing machine will oppress and torture with impunity all the other peoples.' We are weaker economically and technically – that is a fact. Therefore are we doomed? No, comrades, I don't believe it, I don't believe the whole of our European culture is doomed to perdition, that capital will destroy it with impunity, will sell it by auction, bleed it white, crush it. I don't believe it. I believe, comrades, and I know by experience and in the light of Marxist theory, that capitalism is living through its last days. Just as a lamp, before its extinction, flares up brightly for the last time and then all at once goes out, so, comrades, has this mighty lamp of capitalism flared up in this terrible bloody slaughter to illuminate the world of violence, oppression, and slavery in which we have hitherto lived, and to cause the toiling masses to shudder in horror and to awake. We revolted, so will the European working class revolt. And then not only the Brest-Litovsk treaty will fly to the very bottom of hell, but a lot of other things, too: all the crowned and uncrowned despots, the imperialist bandits and usurers, and a reign of liberty and fraternity among all peoples will ensue.

17. Lenin Wounded

On August 30, 1918 a Social Revolutionary, Dora Kaplan, attempted to assassinate Lenin. Trotsky rushed back to Moscow from the front line on the Volga and gave this speech to the All-Russian Central Executive Committee of the Soviets.

Comrades, your brotherly greetings I explain by the fact that in these difficult days and hours we all feel deeply as brothers a need of closer union with each other and with our Soviet organizations, and the need of closing our ranks more tightly under our Communist banner.

In these days and hours so filled with anxiety, when our standard-bearer, and with perfect right it can be said the international standard-bearer of the proletariat, lies on his sickbed fighting with the terrible shadow of death, we are drawn closer to one another than in the hours of victory . . .

The news of the attack on Comrade Lenin reached me and many other comrades in Svyazhsk on the Kazan front. We suffered blows there, blows from the right, blows from the left, blows between the eyes. But this new blow was a blow in the back from ambush deep in the rear. This treacherous blow has opened a new front, which for the present moment is the most distressing, the most alarming for us: the front where Vladimir Ilyich's life struggles with death. Whatever defeats may await us on this or that front – and I am like you firmly convinced of our imminent victory – no single partial defeat could be so onerous, so tragic, for the working class of Russia and the whole world, as would be a fatal issue of the fight at the front that runs through the breast of our leader.

One need only reflect in order to understand the concentrated hate that this figure has called forth and will continue to call forth from all the enemies of the working class. For nature produced a masterpiece when it created in a single individual an embodiment of the revolutionary thought and the unbending energy of the working class. This figure is Vladimir Ilyich Lenin. The gallery of proletarian leaders, revolutionary fighters, is very rich and varied, and like many other comrades who have been in revolutionary work for three decades,

I have had the opportunity to meet in different lands many varieties of the proletarian type of leader – the revolutionary representatives of the working class. But only in the person of Comrade Lenin have we a figure created for our epoch of blood and iron.

Behind us lies the epoch of so-called peaceful development of bourgeois society, during which contradictions accumulated gradually, while Europe lived through the period of so-called armed peace, and blood flowed almost in the colonies alone where predatory capital tortured the more backward peoples. Europe enjoyed her so-called peace of capitalist militarism. In this epoch were formed and fashioned the outstanding leaders of the European working-class movement. Among them we saw such a brilliant figure as that of August Bebel. But he reflected the epoch of the gradual and slow development of the working class. Along with courage and iron energy, the most extreme caution in all moves, the painstaking probing of the ground, the strategy of watchful waiting and preparation were peculiar to him. He reflected the process of the gradual molecular accumulation of the forces of the working class – his thought advanced step by step, just as the German working class in the epoch of world reaction rose only gradually from the depths, freeing itself from darkness and prejudices. His spiritual figure grew, developed, became stronger and rose in stature – but all this took place on the selfsame ground of watchful waiting and preparation. Such was August Bebel in his ideas and methods – the best figure of an epoch which lies behind us and which already belongs to eternity.

Our epoch is woven of different material. This is the epoch when the old accumulated contradictions have led to a monstrous explosion, and have torn asunder the integument of bourgeois society. In this epoch all the foundations of world capitalism are being shattered to the ground by the holocaust of the European peoples. It is the epoch which has revealed all the class contradictions and has confronted the popular masses with the horrible reality of the destruction of millions in the name of the naked greed for profits. And it is for this epoch that the history of Western Europe has forgotten, neglected, or failed to bring about the creation of *the* leader – and this was not due to chance: for all the leaders who on the eve of the war enjoyed the greatest confidence of the European working class reflected its past but not its present . . .

And when the new epoch came, this epoch of terrible convulsions and bloddy battles, it went beyond the strength of the earlier leaders. It pleased history – and not by accident! – to create a figure at a single casting in Russia, a figure that reflects in itself our entire harsh and great epoch. I repeat that this is no accident. In 1847, backward Germany produced from its milieu the figure of Karl Marx, the greatest of all fighters and thinkers, who anticipated and pointed out the paths to new history. Germany was then a backward country, but history willed it that Germany's intelligentsia of that time should go through a revolutionary development and that the greatest representative of this intelligentsia, enriched by their entire scientific knowledge, should break with bourgeois society, place himself on the side of the revolutionary proletariat, and work out the programme of the workers' movement and the theory of development of the working class.

What Marx prophesied in that epoch, our epoch is called upon to carry out. But for this, our epoch needs new leaders who must be the bearers of the great spirit of our epoch in which the working class has risen to the heights of its historic task, and sees clearly the great frontier that it must pass if mankind is to live and not rot like carrion on the main highway of history. For this epoch Russian history has created a new leader. All that was best in the old revolutionary intelligentsia of Russia, their spirit of self-denial, their audacity and hatred of oppression, all this has been concentrated in this figure, who, in his youth, however, broke irrevocably with the world of the intelligentsia on account of their connection with the bourgeoisie, and embodied in himself the meaning and substance of the development of the working class. Relying on the young revolutionary proletariat of Russia, utilizing the rich experience of the world working-class movement, transforming its ideology into a lever for action, this figure has today risen in its full stature on the political horizon. It is the figure of Lenin, the greatest man of our revolutionary epoch.

I know, and you know too, comrades, that the fate of the working class does not depend on single personalities; but that does not mean that personality is a matter of indifference in the history of our movement and in the development of the working class. A personality cannot model the working class in his own image and after his likeness, nor point out to the proletariat arbitrarily this or that path of development, but he can help the fulfilment of the workers' tasks and lead them more quickly to their goal. The critics of Karl Marx have pointed out that he forecast the revolution much sooner than was actually the case. The critics were answered with perfect right that inasmuch as Marx stood on a lofty peak, the distances seemed shorter to him.

Many including myself have criticized Vladimir Ilyich too, more than once, for seemingly failing to take into account many secondary causes and concomitant circumstances. I must say that this might have been a defect for a political leader in an epoch of 'normal' gradual development; but this is the greatest merit of Comrade Lenin as leader of the new epoch, during which all that is concomitant, superficial, and secondary falls away and recedes to the background, leaving only the basic, irreconcilable antagonism of the classes in the fearful form of civil war. To fix his revolutionary sight upon the future, to grasp and point out the most important, the fundamental, the most urgently needed – that was the gift peculiar to Lenin in the highest degree. Those to whom it was granted, as it was to me in this period, to observe Vladimir Ilyich at work and the workings of his mind at close range could not fail to greet with open and immediate enthusiasm – I repeat, with enthusiasm – the gift of the penetrating, piercing mind that rejected all the external, the accidental, the superficial, in order to mark out the main roads and methods of action. The working class is learning to value only those leaders who, after uncovering the path of development, follow it without hesitation, even when the prejudices of the proletariat itself become temporarily an obstacle along this path. In addition to this gift of a powerful mind Vladimir Ilyich also was endowed with an inflexible will. And the combination of these qualities produces the real revolutionary leader, who is the fusion of a courageous, unwavering mind and a steeled and inflexible will.

What good fortune it is that all that we say, hear, and read in our resolutions on Lenin is not in the form of an obituary. And yet we came so near that ... We are convinced that on this near front, here in the Kremlin, life will conquer and Vladimir Ilyich will soon return to our ranks.

I have said, comrades, that he embodies the courageous mind and revolutionary will of the working class. One ought to say that there is an inner symbol, almost a conscious design of history in this, that our leader in these difficult hours when the Russian working class fights on the outer front with all its strength against the Czechoslovaks, the White Guards, the mercenaries of England and France – that our leader is fighting those wounds which were inflicted on him by the agents of these very White Guards, Czechoslovaks, the mercenaries of England and France. In this is an inner connection and a deep historical symbol! And just as we are all convinced that in our struggle on the Czechoslovak, Anglo-French, and White Guard front we are growing stronger every day and every hour – I can state that as an eyewitness who has just returned from the military arena, yes, we grow stronger every day, we shall be stronger tomorrow than we are today, and stronger the day after than we shall be tomorrow; I have no doubt that the day is not distant when we can say to you that Kazan, Simbirsk, Samara, Ufa, and the other temporarily occupied cities have returned to our Soviet family – in exactly the same way we are hopeful that the process of recovery of Comrade Lenin will be swift.

But even now his image, the inspiring image of our wounded leader who has left the front for a time, stands clearly before us. We know that not for a moment has he left our ranks, for, even when laid low by treacherous bullets, he rouses us all, summons us, and drives us onward. I have not seen a single comrade, nor a single honest worker, who let his hands drop under the influence of the news of the traitorous attack on Lenin, but I have seen scores who clenched their fists, whose hands sought their guns; I have heard hundreds and thousands of lips that vowed merciless revenge on the class enemies of the proletariat. You need hardly be told how the class-conscious fighters at the front reacted when they learned that Lenin was lying with two bullets in his body. No one can say of Lenin that his character lacks metal; but now there is metal not only in his spirit, but in his body, and thereby he is even dearer to the working class of Russia.

I do not know if our words and heartbeats can now reach Lenin's sickbed, but I have no doubt that he senses them. I have no doubt that he knows even in his fever how our hearts too beat in double, threefold measure. We all realize now more clearly than ever that we are members of a single Communist Soviet family. Never did the life of each of us seem such a secondary or tertiary thing as it does at the moment when the life of the greatest man of our time is in mortal danger. Any fool can shoot a bullet through Lenin's head, but to create this head anew – that is a difficult task even for nature itself.

But no, he will soon be up again, to think and to create, to fight side by side with us. In return we promise our beloved leader that as long as any mental power remains in our own heads, and blood runs through our hearts, we shall remain true to the banner of the Communist revolution. We shall fight against the enemies of the working class to the last drop of blood, to our last breath.

In Exile

18. I Stake My Life!

Having been first marginalised and then expelled by Stalin, Trotsky was banished from Moscow to Alma-Ata and then lived in the 1930s in Turkey, France, Norway and Mexico, generally under severe restraints. In the wake of the Moscow Show Trials Trotsky was invited to address the American Committee for the Defense of Leon Trotsky at a mass meeting in New York on February 9, 1937. When Trotsky was refused a visa, the speech was read out on his behalf.

My first word is one of apology for my impossible English. My second word is one of thanks to the committee which has made it possible for me to address your meeting. The theme of my address is the Moscow trials. I do not intend for an instant to overstep the limits of this theme, which even in itself is much too vast. I will appeal not to the passions, not to your nerves, but to reason. I do not doubt that *reason* will be found on the side of *truth*.

The Zinoviev–Kamenev trial has provoked in public opinion, terror, agitation, indignation, distrust, or at least, perplexity. The trial of Pyatakov–Radek has once more enhanced these sentiments. Such is the incontestable fact. A doubt of justice signifies, in this case, a suspicion of frame-up. Can one find a more humiliating suspicion against a government which appears under the banner of socialism? Where do the interests of the Soviet government itself lie? In dispelling these suspicions. What is the duty of the true friends of the Soviet Union? To say firmly to the Soviet government: it is necessary at all costs to dispel the distrust of the Western world for Soviet justice.

To answer to this demand: 'We have our justice, the rest does not concern us much,' is to occupy oneself, not with the Socialist enlightenment of the masses, but with the policies of inflated prestige, in the style of Hitler or Mussolini.

Even the 'friends of the USSR', who are convinced in their own hearts of the justice of the Moscow trials (and how many are there? What a pity that one cannot take a census of consciences!), even these unshakeable friends of the bureaucracy are duty-bound to demand with us the creation of an authorized commission of inquiry. The Moscow authorities must present to such a commission all the necessary testimonies. There can evidently be no lack of them, since it was on the basis of those given that forty-nine persons were shot in the 'Kirov' trials, without counting the 150 who were shot without trial.

Let us recall that by way of guarantees for the justice of the Moscow verdicts before world public opinion, two lawyers present themselves: Pritt from London and Rosenmark from Paris, not to mention the American journalist Duranty. But who gives guarantee for these guarantees? The two lawyers Pritt and Rosenmark acknowledge gratefully that the Soviet government placed at their disposal all the necessary explanations. Let us add that the 'king's counsellor' Pritt was invited to Moscow at a fortunate time, since the date of the trial was carefully concealed from the entire world until the last moment. The Soviet government did not thus count on humiliating the dignity of its justice by having recourse behind the scenes to the assistance of foreign lawyers and journalists. But when the Socialist and Trade Union Internationals demanded the opportunity to send their lawyers to Moscow, they were treated – no more and no less – as defenders of assassins and of the Gestapo! You know, of course, that I am not a partisan of the Second International or of the Trade Union International. But is it not clear that their moral authority is incomparably above the authority of lawyers with supple spines? Have we not the right to say: the Moscow government forgets its 'prestige' before authorities and experts, whose approbation is assured to them in advance; it is cheerfully willing to make the 'king's counsellor' Pritt a counsellor of the GPU. But, on the other hand, it has up to now brutally rejected every examination which would carry with it guarantees of objectivity and impartiality. Such is the incontestable and deadly fact! Perhaps, however, this conclusion is inaccurate? There is nothing easier than to refute it: let the Moscow government present to an international commission of inquiry serious, precise, and concrete explanations regarding all the obscure spots of the Kirov trials. And apart from these obscure spots there is – alas! – nothing! That is precisely why Moscow resorts to all kinds of measures to force me, the principal accused, to keep my silence. Under Moscow's terrible economic pressure the Norwegian government placed me under lock and key. What good fortune that the magnanimous hospitality of Mexico permitted myself and my wife to meet the new trial, not under imprisonment, but in freedom! But all the wheels to force me once more into silence have again been set into motion. Why does Moscow so fear the voice of a single man? Only because I know the truth, the whole truth. Only because I have nothing to hide. Only because I am ready to appear before a public and impartial commission of inquiry with documents, facts, and testimonies in my hands, and to disclose the truth to the very end. *I declare: if this commission decides that I am guilty in the slightest degree of the crimes which Stalin imputes to me, I pledge in advance to place myself voluntarily in the hands of the executioners of the GPU.* That, I hope, is clear. Have you all heard? I make this declaration before the entire world. I ask the press to publish my words in the farthest corners of our planet. But if the commission establishes – do you hear me? – that the Moscow trials are a conscious and pre-meditated frame-up, constructed with the bones and nerves of human beings, I will not ask my accusers to place themselves voluntarily before a firing squad. No, the eternal disgrace in the memory of human generations will be sufficient for them! Do the accusers of the Kremlin hear me? I throw my defiance in their faces. And I await their reply!

Through this declaration I reply in passing to the frequent objections of superficial sceptics: 'Why must we believe

Trotsky and not Stalin?' It is absurd to busy one's self with psychological divinations. It is not a question of personal confidence. It is a question of *verification!* I propose a verification! I demand the verification!

Listeners and friends! Today you expect from me neither a refutation of the 'proofs', which do not exist in this affair, nor a detailed analysis of the 'confessions', those *unnatural*, artificial, inhuman monologues which carry in themselves their own refutation. I would need more time than the prosecutor for a concrete analysis of the trials, because it is more difficult to disentangle than to entangle. This work I will accomplish in the press and before the future commission. My task today is to unmask the *fundamental, original* viciousness of the Moscow trials, to show the motive forces of the frame-up, its true political aims, the psychology of its participants and of its victims.

The trial of Zinoviev–Kamenev was concentrated upon 'terrorism'. The trial of Pyatakov–Radek placed in the centre of the stage, no longer terror, but the alliance of the Trotskyists with Germany and Japan for the preparation of war, the dismemberment of the USSR, the sabotage of industry, and the extermination of workers. How to explain this crying discrepancy? For, after the execution of the sixteen we were told that the depositions of Zinoviev, Kamenev, and the others were voluntary, sincere, and corresponded to the facts. Moreover, Zinoviev and Kamenev demanded the death penalty for themselves! Why then did they not say a word about the most important thing: the alliance of the Trotskyists with Germany and Japan and the plot to dismember the

USSR? Could they have forgotten such 'details' of the plot? Could they themselves, the leaders of the so-called *centre*, not have known what was known by the accused in the last trial, people of a secondary category? The enigma is easily explained: the new amalgam was constructed *after* the execution of the sixteen, during the course of the last five months, as an answer to unfavourable echoes in the world press.

The most feeble part of the trial of the sixteen is the accusation against Old Bolsheviks of an alliance with the secret police of Hitler, the Gestapo. Neither Zinoviev, nor Kamenev, nor Smirnov, nor in general any one of the accused with political names, confessed to this liaison; they stopped short before this extreme of self-abasement! It follows that I, through obscure, unknown intermediaries such as Olberg, Berman, Fritz David and others, had entered into an alliance with the Gestapo for such grand purposes as the obtaining of a Honduran passport for Olberg. The whole thing was too foolish. No one wanted to believe it. The whole trial was discredited. It was necessary to correct the gross error of the stage managers at all costs. It was necessary to fill up the hole. Yagoda was replaced by Yezhov. A new trial was placed on the order of the day. Stalin decided to answer his critics in this way: 'You don't believe that Trotsky is capable of entering into alliance with the Gestapo for the sake of an Olberg and a passport from Honduras? Very well, I will show you that the purpose of his alliance with Hitler was to provoke war and partition out the world.' However, for this second, more grandiose production, Stalin lacked the principal actors: he had shot them. In the principal roles of the principal presentation he could place only secondary actors! It is not superfluous to note that Stalin attached much value to Pyatakov and Radek as collaborators. But he had no other people with well-known names, who, if only because of their distant pasts, could pass as 'Trotskyists'. That is why fate descended sternly upon Radek and Pyatakov. The version about my meetings with the rotten trash of the Gestapo through unknown, occasional intermediaries was dropped. The matter was suddenly raised to the heights of the world stage! It was no longer a question of a Honduran passport, but of the parcelling of the USSR and even the defeat of the United States of America. With the aid of a gigantic elevator the plot ascends during a period of five months from the dirty police dregs to the heights on which are decided the destinies of nations. Zinoviev, Kamenev, Smirnov, Mrachkovsky went to their graves without knowing of these grandiose schemes, alliances, and perspectives. Such is the *fundamental falsehood* of the last amalgam!

In order to hide, even if only slightly, the glaring contradiction between the two trials, Pyatakov and Radek testified, under the dictation of the GPU, that they had formed a *'parallel'* centre, in view of Trotsky's lack of confidence in Zinoviev and Kamenev. It is difficult to imagine a more stupid and deceitful explanation! I really did not have confidence in Zinoviev and Kamenev after their capitulation, and I have had no connection with them since 1927. But I had still less confidence in Radek and Pyatakov! Already in 1929 Radek delivered into the hands of the GPU the Oppositionist Blumkin, who was shot silently and without trial. Here is what I wrote then in the Russian *Bulletin of the Opposition*, which appears abroad: 'After having lost the last remnants of his moral equilibrium, Radek does not stop at anything.' It is outrageous to be forced to cite such harsh statements about the unfortunate victims of Stalin. But it would be criminal to hide the truth out of sentimental considerations ... Radek and Pyatakov themselves regarded Zinoviev and Kamenev as their superiors, and in this self-appreciation they were not mistaken. But more than that. At the time of the trial of the sixteen, the prosecutor named Smirnov as the 'leader of the Trotskyites in the USSR'. The accused Mrachkovsky, as a proof of his proximity to me, declared that I was accessible only through his intermediation, and the prosecutor in his turn emphasized this fact. How then was it possible that not only Zinoviev and Kamenev, but Smirnov, the 'leader of the Trotskyists in the USSR', and Mrachkovsky as well, knew nothing of the plans about which I had instructed Radek, openly branded by me as a traitor? Such is the primary falsehood of the last trial. It appears by itself in broad daylight. We know its source. We see the strings off stage. We see the brutal hand which pulls them.

Radek and Pyatakov confessed to frightful crimes. But their crimes, from the point of view of the accused and not of the accusers, *do not make sense*. With the aid of terror, sabotage and alliance with the imperialists, they would have liked to re-establish capitalism in the Soviet Union. Why? Throughout their entire lives they struggled against capitalism. Perhaps they were guided by personal motives: the lust for power? the thirst for gain? Under any other regime Pyatakov and Radek could not hope to occupy higher positions than those which they occupied before their arrest. Perhaps they were so stupidly sacrificing themselves out of friendship for me? An absurd hypothesis! By their actions, speeches, and articles during the last eight years, Radek and Pyatakov demonstrated that they were my bitter enemies.

Terror? But is it possible that the Oppositionists, after all the revolutionary experience in Russia, could not have foreseen that this would only serve as a pretext for the extermination of the best fighters? No, they knew that, they foresaw it, they stated it hundreds of times. No, terror was not necessary for us. On the other hand it was absolutely necessary for the ruling clique. On March 4, 1929, eight years ago, I wrote: 'Only one thing is left for Stalin: to attempt to draw a line of blood between the official party and the Opposition. He absolutely must *connect the Opposition with attempts at assassination, the preparation of armed insurrection, etc.*' Remember: Bonapartism has never existed in history without police fabrication of plots!

The Opposition would have to be composed of cretins to think that an alliance with Hitler or the Mikado, both of whom are doomed to defeat in the next war, that such an absurd, inconceivable, senseless alliance could yield to revolutionary Marxists anything but disgrace and ruin. On the other hand, such an alliance – of the Trotskyists with Hitler – was most necessary for Stalin. Voltaire says: 'If God did not exist, it would be necessary to invent him.' The GPU says: 'If the alliance does not exist, it is necessary to fabricate it.'

At the heart of the Moscow trials is an absurdity. According to the official version, the Trotskyists had been organizing the most monstrous plot since 1931. However, all of them, as if by command, spoke and wrote in one way but acted in another. In spite of the hundreds of persons implicated in the plot, over a period of five years, not a trace of it was revealed: no splits, no denunciations, no confiscated letters, until the hour of the general confessions arrived! Then a new miracle came to pass. People who had organized assassinations, prepared war, divided the Soviet Union, these hardened criminals suddenly confessed in August 1936 not under the pressure of proofs – no, because there were no proofs – but for certain mysterious reasons, which hypocritical psychologists declare are peculiar attributes of the 'Russian soul'. Just think: yesterday they carried out railroad-wrecking and poisoning of workers – by unseen order of Trotsky. Today they are Trotsky's accusers and heap upon him their pseudocrimes. Yesterday they dreamed only of killing Stalin. Today they all sing hymns of praise to him. What is it: a madhouse? No, the Messieurs Duranty tell us, it is not a madhouse, but the 'Russian soul'. You lie, gentlemen, about the Russian soul. You lie about the human soul in general.

The miracle consists not only in the simultaneity and the universality of the confessions. The miracle, above all, is that, according to the general confessions, the conspirators did something which was fatal precisely to their own political interests, but extremely useful to the leading clique. Once more the conspirators before the tribunal said just what the most servile agents of Stalin would have said. Normal people, following the dictates of their own will, would never have been able to conduct themselves as Zinoviev, Kamenev, Radek, Pyatakov, and the others did. Devotion to their ideas, political dignity, the simple instinct of self-preservation would force them to struggle for themselves, for their personalities, for their interests, for their lives. The only reasonable and fitting question is this: *Who led these people into a state in which all human reflexes are destroyed, and how did he do it?* There is a very simple principle in jurisprudence, which holds the key to many secrets: *id fecit cui prodest;* he who benefits by it, he is the guilty one. The entire conduct of the accused has been dictated from beginning to end, not by their own ideas and interests, but by the interests of the ruling clique. And the pseudoplot, and the confessions, the theatrical judgement and the entirely real executions, all were arranged by one and the same hand. Whose? *Cui prodest?* Who benefits? The hand of Stalin! The rest is deceit, falsehood, and idle babbling about the 'Russian soul'! In the trials there did not figure fighters, nor conspirators, but puppets in the hands of the GPU. They play assigned roles. The aim of the disgraceful performance: to eliminate the whole Opposition, to poison the very source of critical thought, to definitively ensconce the totalitarian regime of Stalin.

We repeat: The accusation is a premeditated frame-up. This frame-up must inevitably appear in each of the defendant's confessions, if they are examined alongside the facts. The prosecutor Vyshinsky knows this very well. That is why he did not address a single concrete question to the accused, which would have embarrassed them considerably. The names, documents, dates, places, means of transportation, circumstances of the meetings – around these decisive facts Vyshinsky has placed a cloak of shame, or to be more exact, a shameless cloak. Vyshinsky dealt with the accused, not in the language of the jurist, but in the conventional language of the past master of frame-up, in the jargon of the thief. The insinuating character of Vyshinsky's questions – along with the complete absence of material proofs – this represents the *second crushing evidence against Stalin*.

But I do not intend to limit myself to these negative proofs. Oh, no! Vyshinsky has not demonstrated and cannot demonstrate that the *subjective confessions* were genuine, that is to say, in harmony with the *objective facts*. I undertake a much more difficult task: to demonstrate that each one of the confessions is false, that is, contradicts reality. Of what do my proofs consist? I will give you a couple of examples. I would need at least an hour to lay before you the two principal episodes: the pseudotrip of the accused Holtzman to see me in Copenhagen, to receive terrorist instructions, and the pseudovoyage of accused Pyatakov to see me in Oslo, to get instructions about the dismemberment of the Soviet Union. I have at my disposal a complete arsenal of proofs that Holtzman did not come to see me in Copenhagen, and that Pyatakov did not come to see me in Oslo. Now I mention only the simplest proofs, all that the limitations of time permit.

Unlike the other defendants, Holtzman indicated the date: November 23–25, 1932 (the secret is simple: through the newspapers it was known when I arrived in Copenhagen) and the following concrete details: Holtzman came to visit me through my son, Leon Sedov, whom he, Holtzman, had met in the Hotel Bristol. Concerning the Hotel Bristol, Holtzman had a previous agreement with Sedov in Berlin. When he came to Copenhagen, Holtzman actually met Sedov in the lobby of this hotel. From there they both came to see me. At the time of Holtzman's rendezvous with me, Sedov, according to Holtzman's words, frequently walked in and out of the room. What vivid details. We sigh in relief: at last we have, not just confused confessions, but also something which looks like a fact. The sad part of it, however, dear listeners, is that my son was not in Copenhagen, neither in November 1932 nor at any other time in his life. I beg you to keep this well in mind! In November 1932, my son was in Berlin, that is, in Germany and not in Denmark, and made vain efforts to leave in order to meet me and his mother in Copenhagen: don't forget that the Weimar democracy was already gasping out its last breath, and the Berlin police were becoming stricter and stricter. All the circumstances of my son's procedure regarding his departure are established by precise evidence. Our daily telephonic communications with my son from Copenhagen to Berlin can be established by the telephone office in Copenhagen. Dozens of witnesses, who at that time surrounded my wife and myself in Copenhagen, knew that we awaited our son impatiently, but in vain. At the same time, all of my son's friends in Berlin know that he attempted in vain to obtain a visa. Thanks precisely to these incessant efforts and obstacles, the fact that the meeting never materialized remains in the memories of dozens of people. They all live abroad and have already given their written depositions. Does that suffice? I should hope so! Pritt and Rosenmark, perhaps, say 'No'? Because they are indulgent only with the GPU! Good: I will meet them halfway. I have still more immediate, still more direct, and still more indisputable proofs. Actually, our meeting with our son took place after we left Denmark, in France, en route to Turkey. That meeting was made possible only thanks to the personal intervention of the French premier at that time, M. Herriot. In the French Ministry of Foreign Affairs my wife's telegram to Herriot, dated the first of December, has been preserved, as well as Herriot's telegraphic instruction to the French consulate in Berlin, on December 3, to give my son a visa immediately. For a time I feared that the agents of the GPU in Paris would seize those documents. Fortunately they have not succeeded. The two telegrams were luckily found some weeks ago in the Ministry of Foreign Affairs. Do you understand me clearly? I now have copies of both telegrams at hand. I do not cite their texts, numbers, and dates in order not to lose any time: I will give them to the press tomorrow. On my son's passport there is a visa granted by the French consulate on December 3. On the morning of the fourth my son left Berlin. On his passport there are seals received at the frontier on the same day. The passport has been preserved in its entirety. Citizens of New York, do you hear my voice from Mexico City? I want you to hear every one of my words, despite my frightful English! Our meeting with our son took place in Paris, in the Gare de Nord, in a second-class train, which took us from Dunkerque, in the presence of dozens of friends who accompanied us and received us. I hope that is enough! Neither the GPU nor Pritt can ignore it. They are gripped in an iron vice. Holtzman could not see my son in Copenhagen because my son was in Berlin. My son could not have gone in and out during the course of the meeting. Who then will believe the fact of the meeting itself? Who will place any credence in the whole confession of Holtzman?

But that isn't all. According to Holtzman's words, his meeting with my son took place, as you have already heard, in the hall of the Hotel Bristol. Magnificent . . . But it so happens that the Hotel Bristol in Copenhagen was razed to its very foundations in 1917! In 1932 this hotel existed only as a fond memory. The hotel was rebuilt only in 1936, precisely during the days when Holtzman was making his unfortunate declarations. The obliging Pritt presents us with the hypothesis of a probable 'slip of the pen': the Russian stenographer, you see, must have heard the word Bristol incorrectly, and moreover, none of the reporting journalists and editors corrected the error. Good! But how about my son? Also a stenographer's slip of the pen? There Pritt, following Vyshinsky, maintains an eloquent silence. In reality the GPU, through its agents in Berlin, knew of my son's efforts and assumed that he met me in Copenhagen. There is the source of the 'slip of the pen'! Holtzman apparently knew the Hotel Bristol through memories of his emigration long ago, and that is why he named it. From that flows the second 'slip of the pen'! Two slips combine to make a catastrophe: of Holtzman's confessions there remains only a cloud of coal dust, as of the Hotel Bristol at the moment of its destruction. And meanwhile – don't forget this! – this is the most important confession in the trial of the sixteen: of all the old revolutionaries, only Holtzman had met with me and received terrorist instructions!

Let us pass to the second episode. Pyatakov came to see me by aeroplane from Berlin to Oslo in the middle of December 1935. Of the thirteen precise questions which I addressed to the Moscow tribunal while Pyatakov was yet alive, not a single one was answered. Each one of these questions destroys Pyatakov's mythical voyage. Meanwhile my Norwegian host, Konrad Knudsen, a parliamentary deputy, and my former secretary, Erwin Wolf, have already stated in the press that I had no Russian visitor in December 1935, and that I made no journeys without them. Don't these depositions satisfy you? Here is another one: the authorities of the Oslo aerodrome have officially established, on the basis of these records, that during the course of December 1935, not a single foreign aeroplane landed at their airport! Perhaps a slip of the pen has also crept into the records of the aerodrome? Master Pritt, enough of your slips of the pen, kindly invent something more intelligent! But your imagination will avail you nothing here: I have at my disposal dozens of direct and indirect testimonies which expose the depositions of the unfortunate Pyatakov, who was forced by the GPU to fly to see me in an imaginary aeroplane, just as the Holy Inquisition forced witches to go to their rendezvous with the devil on a broomstick. The technique has changed, but the essence is the same.

In the Hippodrome there are undoubtedly competent jurists. I beg them to direct their attention to the fact that neither Holtzman nor Pyatakov gave the slightest indication of my address, that is to say, of the time and the meeting place. Neither one nor the other told of the precise passport or the precise name under which he travelled abroad. The prosecutor did not even question them about their passports. The reason is clear: their names would not be found in the lists of travellers abroad. Pyatakov could not have avoided sleeping over in Norway, because the December days are very short. However, he did not name any hotel. The prosecutor did not even question him about the hotel. Why? Because the ghost of the Hotel Bristol hovers over Vyshinsky's head! The prosecutor is not a prosecutor, but Pyatakov's inquisitor and inspirer, just as Pyatakov is only the unfortunate victim of the GPU.

I could now present an enormous amount of testimony and documents which would demolish at their very foundations the confessions of a whole series of defendants: Smirnov, Mrachkovsky, Dreitzer, Radek, Vladimir Romm, Olberg, in short, of all those who tried in the slightest degree to give facts, circumstances of time and place. Such a job, however, can be done successfully only before a commission of inquiry, with the participation of jurists having the necessary time for a detailed examination of documents and for hearing the depositions of witnesses.

But already what has been said by me permits, I hope,

a forecast of the future development of the investigation. On the one hand, an accusation which is fantastic to its very core; the entire old generation of Bolsheviks is accused of an abominable treason, devoid of sense or purpose. To establish this accusation the prosecutor does not have at his command any material proofs, in spite of the thousands and thousands of arrests and searchings. *The complete absence of evidence is the most terrible evidence against Stalin!* The executions are based exclusively on forced confessions. And when facts are mentioned in these confessions, they crumble to dust at the first contact with critical examination.

The GPU is not only guilty of frame-up. It is guilty of concocting a rotten, gross, foolish frame-up. Impunity is depraving. The absence of control paralyses criticism. The falsifiers carry out their work no matter how. They rely on the sum-total effect of confessions and ... executions. If one carefully compares the fantastic nature of the accusation in its entirety with the manifest falsehood of the factual depositions, what is left of all these monotonous confessions? The suffocating odour of the inquisitorial tribunal, and nothing more!

But there is another kind of evidence which seems to me no less important. In the year of my deportation and the eight years of my emigration I wrote to close and distant friends about 2,000 letters, dedicated to the most vital questions of current politics. The letters received by me and the copies of my replies exist. Thanks to their continuity, these letters reveal, above all, the profound contradictions, anachronisms, and direct absurdities of the accusation, not only insofar as myself and my son are concerned, but also as regards the other accused. However, the importance of these letters extends beyond that fact. All of my theoretical and political activity during these years is reflected without a gap in these letters. The letters supplement my books and articles. The examination of my correspondence, it seems to me, is of decisive importance for the characterization of the political and moral personality – not only of myself, but also of my correspondents. Vyshinsky has not been able to present a single letter to the tribunal. I will present to the commission or to a tribunal thousands of letters, addressed, moreover, to the people who are closest to me and from whom I had nothing to hide, particularly to my son, Leon. This correspondence alone by its internal force of conviction nips the Stalinist amalgam in the bud. The prosecutor with his subterfuges and his insults and the accused with their confessional monologues are left suspended in thin air. Such is the significance of my correspondence. Such is the content of my archives. I do not ask anybody's confidence. I make an appeal to reason, to logic, to criticism. I present facts and documents. I demand a verification!

Among you, dear listeners, there must be not a few people who freely say: 'The confessions of the accused are false, that is clear; but how was Stalin able to obtain such confessions; therein lies the secret!' In reality the secret is not so profound. The Inquisition, with a much more simple technique, extorted all sorts of confessions from its victims. That is why the democratic penal law renounced the methods of the Middle Ages, because they led not to the establishment of the truth, but to a simple confirmation of the accusations dictated by the inquiring judge. The GPU trials have a thoroughly inquisitorial character: that is the simple secret of the confessions!

The whole political atmosphere of the Soviet Union is impregnated with the spirit of the Inquisition. Have you read Andre Gide's little book, *Return from the USSR*? Gide is a friend of the Soviet Union, but not a lackey of the bureaucracy. Moreover, this artist has eyes. A little episode in Gide's book is of incalculable aid in understanding the Moscow trials. At the end of his trip Gide wished to send a telegram to Stalin, but not having received the inquisitorial education, he referred to Stalin with the simple democratic word 'you'. They refused to accept the telegram! The representatives of authority explained to Gide: 'When writing to Stalin one must say: "leader of the workers" or "chieftain of the people," not the simple democratic word "you".' Gide tried to argue: 'Isn't Stalin above such flattery?' It was no use. They still refused to accept his telegram without the Byzantine flattery. At the very end Gide declared: 'I submit in this wearisome battle, but disclaim all responsibility . . .' Thus a universally recognized writer and honoured guest was worn out in a few minutes and forced to sign not the telegram which he himself wanted to send, but that which was dictated to him by petty inquisitors. Let him who has a particle of imagination picture to himself, not a well-known traveller but an unfortunate Soviet citizen, an Oppositionist, isolated and persecuted, a pariah, who is constrained to write, not telegrams of salutation to

Stalin, but dozens and scores of confessions of his crimes. Perhaps in this world there are many heroes who are capable of bearing all kinds of tortures, physical or moral, which are inflicted on themselves, their wives, their children. I do not know ... My personal observations inform me that the capacities of the human nervous system are limited. Through the GPU Stalin can trap his victim in an abyss of black despair, humiliation, infamy, in such a manner that he takes upon himself the most monstrous crimes, with the prospect of imminent death or a feeble ray of hope for the future as the sole outcome. If, indeed, he does not contemplate suicide, which Tomsky preferred! Joffe earlier found the same way out, as well as two members of my military secretariat, Glazman and Boutov, Zinoviev's secretary, Bogdan, my daughter Zinaida, and many dozens of others. Suicide or moral prostration: there is no other choice! But do not forget that in the prisons of the GPU even suicide is often an inaccessible luxury!

The Moscow trials do not dishonour the revolution, because they are the progeny of reaction. The Moscow trials do not dishonour the old generation of Bolsheviks; they only demonstrate that even Bolsheviks are made of flesh and blood, and that they do not resist endlessly when over their heads swings the pendulum of death. The Moscow trials dishonour the political regime which has conceived them: the regime of Bonapartism, without honour and without conscience! All of the executed died with curses on their lips for this regime.

Let him who wishes weep bitter tears because history moves ahead so perplexingly: two steps forward, one step back. But tears are of no avail. It is necessary, according to Spinoza's advice, not to laugh, not to weep, but to understand!

Who are the principal defendants? Old Bolsheviks, builders of the party, of the Soviet state, of the Red Army, of the Communist International. Who is the accuser against them? *Vyshinsky*, bourgeois lawyer, who called himself a Menshevik after the October Revolution and joined the Bolsheviks after their definitive victory. Who wrote the disgusting libels about the accused in *Pravda*? *Zaslavsky*, former pillar of a banking journal, whom Lenin treated in his articles only as a 'rascal'. The former editor of *Pravda*, Bukharin, is arrested. The pillar of *Pravda* is now *Koltzov*, bourgeois feuilletonist, who remained throughout the civil war in the camp of the Whites. *Sokolnikov*, a participant in the October Revolution and the civil war, is condemned as a traitor. *Rakovsky* awaits accusation. Sokolnikov and Rakovsky were ambassadors to London. Their place is now occupied by *Maisky*, Right Menshevik, who during the civil war was a minister of the White government in Kolchak's territory. *Troyanovsky*, Soviet ambassador to Washington, treats the Trotskyists as counter-revolutionaries. He himself during the first years of the October Revolution was a member of the Central Committee of the Mensheviks and joined the Bolsheviks only after they began to distribute attractive posts. Before becoming ambassador, Sokolnikov was people's commissar of finance. Who occupies that post today? *Grinko*, who in common with the White Guards struggled in the Committee of Welfare during 1917–18 against the Soviets. One of the best Soviet diplomatists was Joffe, first ambassador to Germany, who was forced to suicide by the persecutions. Who replaced him in Berlin? First the repented Oppositionist Krestinski, then *Khinchuk*, former Menshevik, a participant in the counter-revolutionary Committee of Welfare, and finally *Suritz*, who also went through 1917 on the other side of the barricades. I could prolong this list indefinitely.

These sweeping alterations in personnel, especially striking in the provinces, have profound social causes. What are they? It is time, my listeners, it is high time, to recognize, finally, that a new aristocracy has been formed in the Soviet Union. The October Revolution proceeded under the banner of equality. The bureaucracy is the embodiment of monstrous inequality. The revolution destroyed the nobility. The bureaucracy creates a new gentry. The revolution destroyed titles and decorations. The new aristocracy produces marshals and generals. The new aristocracy absorbs an enormous part of the national income. Its position before the people is deceitful and false. Its leaders are forced to hide the reality, to deceive the masses, to cloak themselves, calling black white. The whole policy of the new aristocracy is a frame-up. The new constitution is nothing but a frame-up.

Fear of criticism is fear of the masses. The bureaucracy is afraid of the people. The lava of the revolution is not yet cold. The bureaucracy cannot crush the discontented and the critics by bloody repressions only because they demand a cutting-down of privileges. That is why the false accusations against the Opposition are not occasional acts but a *system*, which flows from the present situation of the ruling caste.

Let us recall how the Thermidorians of the French Revolution acted toward the Jacobins. The historian Aulard writes: 'The enemies did not satisfy themselves with the assassination of Robespierre and his friends; they calumniated them, representing them in the eyes of France as royalists, as people who had sold out to foreign countries.' Stalin has invented nothing. He has simply replaced royalists with fascists.

When the Stalinists call us 'traitors', there is in that accusation not only hatred but also a certain sort of sincerity. They think that we betray the interests of the holy caste of generals and marshals, the only ones capable of 'constructing socialism', but who in fact compromise the very idea of socialism. For our part, we consider the Stalinists as traitors to the interests of the Soviet masses and of the world proletariat. It is absurd to explain such a furious struggle by personal motives. It is a question not only of different programmes, but also of different social interests, which clash in an increasingly hostile fashion.

'And what is your general diagnosis?' you will ask me. 'What is your prognosis?' I said before: My speech is devoted only to the Moscow trials. The social diagnosis and prognosis form the content of my new book: *The Revolution Betrayed: What Is the Soviet Union and Where Is It Going?* But in two words I will tell you what I think.

The fundamental acquisitions of the October Revolution, the new forms of property which permit the development of the productive forces, are not yet destroyed, but they have already come into irreconcilable conflict with the political despotism. Socialism is impossible without the independent activity of the masses and the flourishing of the human personality. Stalinism tramples on both. An open revolutionary conflict between the people and the new despotism is inevitable. Stalin's regime is doomed. Will the capitalist counter-revolution or workers' democracy replace it? History has not yet decided this question. The decision depends also upon the activity of the world proletariat.

If we admit for a moment that fascism will triumph in Spain, and thereby also in France, the Soviet country, surrounded by a fascist ring, would be doomed to further degeneration, which must extend from the political superstructure to the economic foundations. In other words, the debacle of the European proletariat would probably signify the crushing of the Soviet Union.

If on the contrary the toiling masses of Spain overcome fascism, if the working class of France definitely chooses the path of its liberation, then the oppressed masses of the Soviet Union will straighten their backbones and raise their heads! Then will the last hour of Stalin's despotism strike. But the triumph of Soviet democracy will not occur by itself. It depends also upon you. The masses need your help. The first aid is to tell them the truth.

The question is: to aid the demoralized bureaucracy against the people, or the progressive forces of the people against the bureaucracy. The Moscow trials are a signal. Woe to them who do not heed! The Reichstag trial surely had a great importance. But it concerned only vile fascism, this embodiment of all the vices of darkness and barbarism. The Moscow trials are perpetrated under the banner of socialism. We will not concede this banner to the masters of falsehood! If our generation happens to be too weak to establish socialism over the earth, we will hand the spotless banner down to our children. The struggle which is in the offing transcends by far the importance of individuals, factions, and parties. It is the struggle for the future of all mankind. It will be severe. It will be lengthy. Whoever seeks physical comfort and spiritual calm, let him step aside. In time of reaction it is more convenient to lean on the bureaucracy than on the truth. But all those for whom the word *socialism* is not a hollow sound but the content of their moral life – forward! Neither threats, nor persecutions, nor violations can stop us! Be it even over our bleaching bones, the truth will triumph! We will blaze the trail for it. It will conquer! Under all the severe blows of fate, I shall be happy, as in the best days of my youth, if together with you I can contribute to its victory! Because, my friends, the highest human happiness is not the exploitation of the present but the preparation of the future.

19. Testament

*Living in Coyoacan in Mexico, Trotsky wrote this short testament
at the end of February and beginning of March 1940. He survived a
major assassination attempt by Stalinist agents in May but
succumbed to a further attempt on August 20.*

My high (and still rising) blood pressure is deceiving
those near me about my actual condition. I am active
and able to work but the outcome is evidently near.
These lines will be made public after my death.

I have no need to refute here once again the stupid
and vile slander of Stalin and his agents: there is not a
single spot on my revolutionary honour. I have never
entered, either directly or indirectly, into any behind-
the-scenes agreements or even negotiations with the
enemies of the working class. Thousands of Stalin's
opponents have fallen victims of similar false accusations. The new revolutionary generations will rehabili-
tate their political honour and deal with the Kremlin
executioners according to their deserts.

I thank warmly the friends who remained loyal to me
through the most difficult hours of my life. I do not name
anyone in particular because I cannot name them all.

However, I consider myself justified in making an
exception in the case of my companion, Natalia Ivanovna
Sedova. In addition to the happiness of being a fighter
for the cause of socialism, fate gave me the happiness of
being her husband. During the almost forty years of our
life together she remained an inexhaustible source of

love, magnanimity, and tenderness. She underwent great sufferings, especially in the last period of our lives. But I find some comfort in the fact that she also knew days of happiness.

For forty-three years of my conscious life I have remained a revolutionist; for forty-two of them I have fought under the banner of Marxism. If I had to begin all over again I would of course try to avoid this or that mistake, but the main course of my life would remain unchanged. I shall die a proletarian revolutionist, a Marxist, a dialectical materialist, and, consequently, an irreconcilable atheist. My faith in the communist future of mankind is not less ardent, indeed it is firmer today, than it was in the days of my youth.

Natasha has just come up to the window from the courtyard and opened it wider so that the air may enter more freely into my room. I can see the bright green strip of grass beneath the wall, and the clear blue sky above the wall, and sunlight everywhere. Life is beautiful. Let the future generations cleanse it of all evil, oppression, and violence and enjoy it to the full.

> *L. Trotsky*
> FEBRUARY 27, 1940
> COYOACAN.

All the possessions remaining after my death, all my literary rights (income from my books, articles, etc.) are to be placed at the disposal of my wife, Natalia Ivanovna Sedova. February 27, 1940. L. Trotsky.

In case we both die [*the rest of the page is blank*]

★

March 3, 1940

The nature of my illness (high and rising blood pressure) is such – as I understand it – that the end must come suddenly, most likely – again, this is my personal hypothesis – through a brain haemorrhage. This is the best possible end I can wish for. It is possible, however, that I am mistaken (I have no desire to read special books on this subject and the physicians naturally will not tell the truth). If the sclerosis should assume a protracted character and I should be threatened with a long-drawn-out invalidism (at present I feel, on the contrary, rather a surge of spiritual energy because of the high blood pressure, but this will not last long), then I reserve the right to determine for myself the time of my death. The 'suicide' (if such a term is appropriate in this connection) will not in any respect be an expression of an outburst of despair or hopelessness. Natasha and I said more than once that one may arrive at such a physical condition that it would be better to cut short one's own life or, more correctly, the too slow process of dying . . . But whatever may be the circumstances of my death I shall die with unshaken faith in the communist future. This faith in man and in his future gives me even now such power of resistance as cannot be given by any religion.

L. Tr